Books by Ved Mehta

John Is Easy to Please

VED MEHTA

JOHN IS EASY TO PLEASE

Encounters with the Written and the Spoken Word

FARRAR, STRAUS & GIROUX

NEW YORK

First printing, 1971
Library of Congress catalog card number: 72-154862
SBN 374.1.7986.7
Published simultaneously in Canada by Doubleday
Canada Ltd., Toronto
Printed in the United States of America
by American Book-Stratford Press, Inc.

Typography & ornament by Guy Fleming

CONTENTS

FOREWORD

I STARTED WRITING FOR *The New Yorker* in 1960, and the six pieces collected here for the first time are gleanings from my ten years of reportorial work for that magazine. They reflect, in different ways, the worlds in which I feel at home: India, where I was born and brought up; the United States and Britain, where I have lived since I was fifteen; and what Milton called "the olive grove of Academe," where I spent an interlude of almost nine years. The pieces are united by the ancient theme of the tongue and the pen; in the words of the Psalm, "My tongue is the pen of a ready writer." George Sherry, the U.N. interpreter ("A Second Voice"); Sir William Haley, the English editor and broadcaster ("The Third"); Sir Basil Blackwell, the Oxford bookman ("Quiet, Beneficent Things"); Ram Babu Saksena, the Urdu translator and critic ("There Is No Telling"); R. K. Narayan, the Indian novelist ("The Train Had Just Arrived at Malgudi Station"); and Noam Chomsky, the American linguist ("John Is Easy to Please")—and many of their confreres who appear in this book—might well be surprised to find themselves in the same room. They would have difficulty in understanding one another's manners, attitudes, and, in some cases, language. The gathering would indeed be a bizarre one—at once flamboyant, Promethean, ironic, romantic, tender, and intellectual—but for me it would be Heaven. After all, as I feel that my autobiography and my other books, taken together, suggest, my whole life is an unprecedented—and so, for the time being, incomprehensible—experiment, conducted by me in the guise of a mad scientist.

V. M.

New York City, January, 1971

I

A Second Voice

A LITTLE WHILE AGO, WHEN I WAS LUNCHING with a friend in the Delegates' Dining Room at the the United Nations headquarters, on the East River, a stranger came up to our table and greeted my companion.

"Hello, George, what's new with you?" my friend said.

"What's *new?*" George retorted, in a loud, raspy voice. "Why, Bongandanga, Bokenda, Lingunda, Balangala, Bolomba, Lulonga, Belondo, Bomputu, Imbonga, Putubumba, Lualaba, Sofumwango, Bolongo, Benungu, Basankusu, Bulukutu, Bokungu, Kingana, Tumbamami, Popokabaka, Ingololo, Bululundu, Mambirima, Musokatanda, Kamatanda, Mulungwishi, Kintobongo, Mukulakulu, Katentania, Tshimbumbula." At the end of this recitation—or, rather, routine—which I recognized somewhere in the middle as a list of names of Congolese towns, he roared with laughter. The newcomer had bright, brown eyes in a pale, round face, made rounder by a prominent forehead and a receding hairline. He was of average height and huskily built, but he didn't give the impression of being a fat man, perhaps because he talked with his whole body—though less in the manner of an actor than in the manner of a prankster. My friend introduced him to me as George Sherry, and after some polite exchanges Sherry walked away.

From my friend I learned that Sherry, who was thirty-eight, was a senior interpreter in the United Nations Interpretation Section, of which he had been a member since 1947, and that soon he would be transferring out of interpretation to the Executive Office of the Secretary-General, to work on political affairs under Ralph Bunche; in fact, my friend said that Sherry was already spending some of his time drafting cables and diplomatic notes for the Secretary-General's Congo staff. Sherry originally joined the Interpretation Section as a précis writer and an editor, but he switched to interpreting almost immediately; now his colleagues regarded him as one of the two or three truly superlative interpreters in memory. Sherry made his mark within days of his arrival. At that time, the U.N. was shifting from the time-consuming system of consecutive interpretation, in which successive interpreters redelivered the original speech in different languages, to simultaneous interpretation, in which the speech would be converted into several other languages sentence by sentence as it went along. Even after the changeover had begun, many of the professionals—who were mostly relics of the League of Nations, and loved remaking delegates' speeches—dismissed the whole idea of a simultaneous transmutation of language, especially if there was no advance text of a speech to work from; the human mind, they said, was incapable of working at such speed. They still saw consecutive interpretation as a great advance over translation (a term interpreters apply only to written conversion of language), and to them the simultaneous method seemed as farfetched as the four-minute mile seemed to ordinary men before Roger Bannister. Then Sherry appeared and began successfully running the four-minute mental mile. His incredible linguistic gifts and dexterous voice took the professionals by surprise, and almost at once that voice started talking English for Andrei Yanuarievich Vishinsky, who was the Soviet Union's permanent delegate to the U.N. from 1945 to 1949 and again in 1953 and 1954. Vishinsky was one of the most difficult speakers to interpret for, because he never followed his text and was given to making rapid speeches full of literary allusions, biting wit, and violent outbursts. For six wordy Cold War years, Sherry had so many opportunities to simultaneously interpret Vishinsky that finally the U.S.S.R. began requesting him for many important meetings, and Sherry started receiving poison-pen letters that accused him of being a soulmate of Vishinsky's. Although Sherry spoke with an almost aggressively American accent, the audience so easily identified the voice with Vishinsky's fulminations that the Secretary-General himself started receiving letters that urged him to get rid of the Communist's twin.

"Without simultaneous interpretation, the U.N. would have to quintuple its meeting time—a human impossibility—and without people like Sherry delegates from different countries couldn't speak to each other," my friend said. "I remember listening to Vishinsky through George's voice. It really was unnerving. You know, Vishinsky made a profession of extemporaneous virtuosity. Well, George's voice worked like an automatic reflex, until one felt that Vishinsky was a double-headed, double-voiced, bilingual monster, simultaneously interpreting himself."

Soon after meeting Sherry, I looked up a few facts about the men who, sentence by sentence, within the space of a few seconds, turn a speech in English, French, Spanish, Russian, or Chinese—the official tongues of the U.N.—into any of the four other languages. I learned that an applicant for the job of interpreter was required to know three of the five languages of the U.N.; that senior interpreters received (before taxes and other deductions) about sixteen thousand dollars a year; that during the plenary sessions of the General Assembly there were altogether approximately seventy interpreters at work; that the interpreters ranged in age from twenty-eight to sixty-one; and that men outnumbered women two to one. Even within an international body like the United Nations, the interpreters were remarkable for their diversity of background. Almost all of them had been bilingual from early childhood, thanks to foreign governesses, foreign schooling, or parents of mixed nationalities. (One interpreter was born in Buenos Aires of a Swiss mother and a Chinese father; another, who eventually married an Australian, had a Russian mother and a French father.) More than half of them had American citizenship, but some held French, Chinese, Argentine, Mexican, English, Belgian, Chilean, Canadian, or Australian passports. Before joining the interpreting service, some of them were teachers, journalists, lawyers, civil servants, film editors, opera producers, or policemen. To discover exactly how one interpreter had developed, I called Sherry up, and he invited me to lunch at his home the following Sunday.

On Sunday, I took a taxi up to West 107th Street, where Sherry and his wife and their six-year-old daughter lived in a five-room apartment. I rang the bell, and Sherry admitted me to a foyer lined with modern, glass-fronted bookcases holding assorted scholarly books in French, Russian, English, and German. Sherry was dressed much as one would expect a U.N. diplomat to be. He was wearing an inconspicuously striped dark-gray suit, a white shirt, and a maroon tie with a woven pattern and fastened to his shirt by a silver tie clip with a small Oriental design; a white handkerchief rose from his breast pocket. We sat down under an abstract painting of a ballet girl in motion.

"My wife, Doris, has taken our daughter, Vivien, to the park," he began. "By the way, 'Vivien' means 'lively,' from the Latin '*vivus*,' and also has a suggestion of hauntedness—from Merlin's Vivien. You know, the magician teaches her a charm, only to be imprisoned in an oak tree by her."

I asked him how he had got started on his linguistic career.

He replied in a rush of mocking words, which rather startled me, because he seemed to be talking about someone else's life. It was as though his voice were still working for some other man. "Like any other boy," he said, a little too loud, "I was born, and had a mother and father, and went to school. There wasn't much to my life until I

7]

touched America, at fifteen. I've never talked about my
birth, but here I come. Catch me. My mother's father
was rich, a minor cotton king, in Lodz, in Poland, who
could afford to have his sensitive only daughter, Henri-
etta—she is a wonderful pianist—educated first in Poland, then in Switzerland, and then at a finishing school
in Margate, England. My father's father, Gregory Szerszewski, who lived in Rostov, on the Don, was an ordinary, middle-class Jewish intellectual. He sold books, and
he wrote poetry and edited a Jewish literary journal. He
begot four sons: Abraham, who grew up to be a lawyer
in Rostov; Ilya, who went on to become an elementary-
school principal; Mendel (I've forgotten what he did);
and Leon, my father, who graduated *s otlichiem*, or
summa cum laude, from the Kharkov Institute of Technology. Although the family remained in Rostov, my
father settled in Kharkov. You might say I started being
born, if not with my grandfathers and their families,
then with the courtship of my mother and father. After
my mother returned to Lodz from England, the First
World War broke out, and she fled with her mother to
Kharkov for safety, and there she met my father. In
1917, she went back home. When, in 1922, my father—
like three million other Russians—also decided to leave
Mother Russia, he discovered that he had another
motherland in Poland. Neither my father nor his father
nor his father nor *his* had ever lived in Poland, but, in
accordance with a Russian law that had to do with
identifying different nationalities, they had always been
described as people from Pinsk. Pinsk, which had been
part of Russia since 1795, was given to Poland in 1918,

so, as a 'man of Pinsk,' Leon was able to move to Lodz, in Poland, and he and my mama got married, and in the course of things I followed—to be exact, on the fifth day of January in the year of our Lord nineteen hundred and twenty-four. After begetting me in Lodz, my father went to Vienna in search of a job. He was taken on by the famous Körting engineering firm, and until the depression, when he went into business for himself, he looked after the Körting office in Bucharest. I therefore passed my whole childhood in the ancient seat of Walachian princes. Bucharest was a relatively modern city, with wide boulevards and overhanging trees. We lived in a seven-room apartment in a four-story building on the Boulevard Elisabeta."

The thing about the apartment that made the deepest impression on Yorik, which is what Sherry was called as a child, was a breakfront in the dining room, which contained porcelain figurines and Meissen, Rosenthal, and Sèvres china. He began to learn German from a German governess, and when he was three his father taught him to read and write Russian, which was the language of the household; two years later, he started on French and English with tutors. When he was six, he began his formal studies, in the Elementary School of the Evangelical Lutheran Community, a private school, where he was taught half the time in Rumanian and the other half in German. Here he fortified his German and picked up Rumanian, but he did not neglect his formal study of Russian. Around his fifteenth birthday—by which time he had learned to annoy his father by calling Russian "the language of Dostoevski," instead of "the language of Tolstoy," which was its favored sobriquet in the household—Hitler cast his shadow over Eastern Europe, and so, when George graduated from the Evangelical School, in 1934, and had to choose between going to a German *Gymnasium* and going to a Rumanian *lycée*, he chose the second. Dressed in khaki knee pants, a khaki jacket, and a cap that had an impressive lacquered visor and was piped in sky blue, the school color, George attended his new school from eight to one, six days a week. "There wasn't much time for mischief," Sherry recalled. "In the afternoons, I was busy with my tutors. On Monday and Thursday, there was French, with Mme. Van Acker. She was an extremely elegant, vivacious, and cultured Frenchwoman who was married to an official of the National Bank of Rumania. Then, on Tuesday and Friday, there was English, with Miss Wisely, whom I can compare only to Miss Prism, in 'The Importance of Being Earnest'; from Miss Wisely I learned the value of understatement, irony, and subtle English-style wit. I passed Wednesday afternoon and Saturday afternoon with Mrs. Papelian, studying the piano. Since we have gone this deep, I may say that Mrs. Papelian was an Armenian, a student of Cortot's, and that she adored Chopin scherzos; she made me practice them an hour a day. In my free time, mostly in the evenings, I would read: things like Gogol's mystery tales; French stories by Jules Verne and Alexandre Dumas; Karl May's German adventure books—he wrote damn well about American Indians and other swashbuckling characters—and anything by Wells. For more serious reading, I had books like the gray cloth 'History of

French Literature,' by Des Granges, which encouraged me to read works by Molière and Racine, and so on, for myself." George's memory developed along with his knowledge of languages, until he found that he could recite pages of poetry by Pushkin and Nekrasov, and could act out whole scenes from Molière. Whenever a schoolmate had a birthday, all the children in the class were given an opportunity to show off, since the favorite entertainment on such occasions was for each child to act a part in a play, recite a poem, or sing a song. "On my eleventh birthday," Sherry said, "I got an extra piece of cake for playing the role of Maître Jacques in 'L'Avare.' "

There was a clatter in the foyer, and Sherry's daughter raced in, singing "Ding, dong, dong, ding." Vivien had light-brown hair worn in bangs, and bright-blue eyes, and seemed to be a boisterous, All-American girl. After hugging her father's knee, she got her tricycle and jingled into her room to play. Her mother, a woman in her middle thirties with the same coloring as Vivien's, came in and greeted us. After a few minutes, she called her mother on the telephone and talked to her first in German and then in another language, unfamiliar to me. "The mysterious gibberish you hear is a pulp of German, Flemish, and French," Sherry explained. "But Doris chauvinistically insists on calling it Luxembourgish. She was born in Luxembourg, and came to New York at the age of fifteen. We met in college, and were married fifteen years ago."

While his wife was preparing lunch, Sherry told me how he had come to America. In 1939, sensing currents of anti-Semitism, the Szerszewskis closed down their prosperous business, converted their capital into foreign currency in the black market, packed their belongings, took a train from Bucharest to Paris, boarded the Queen Mary, and, on June 18th, arrived in America. In New York, they moved into a three-room apartment on West Ninety-ninth Street that a Rumanian friend found for them; reconciled themselves to a drop in their standard of living; and changed the name Szerszewski to Sherry.

Mrs. Sherry called us to the dining room for lunch. The meal, which consisted principally of cold cuts, was a clamorous affair, with Vivien talking most of the time and Mrs. Sherry making frequent trips between the well-stocked refrigerator and the table. There wasn't a hint of Europe anywhere; the lunch could have been taking place in any American home. Over a plate of tongue, corned beef, stuffed eggs, and rolls, Sherry talked about his American school days. "As soon as I arrived in the States, I entered Townsend Harris, one of the City College of New York preparatory schools," he said. "I spent three years there and then went on to City College. It was an excellent school."

"Didn't you miss your European tutors?" I asked.

"Never," he replied. "I had other things to think about."

"With your knowledge of Russian, French, German, and Rumanian, you must have felt quite superior to the other children," I said. "You must have been at the head of your class."

"Not at all," he said. "I had to brush up on my English. Anyway, knowing languages has nothing to do with intelligence, advancement, studies. Sometimes I did read my assignments in foreign languages, but otherwise I was just like any other kid."

I inquired how Sherry had got on during these early years in America.

"America?" he said. "Took to it like a duck to water. I loved everything about it from the start, and have always found it the best place in the world."

"Have you ever returned to Eastern Europe?" I asked.

"Yes, but only to Russia," he said. "Quite recently, at the Second Unofficial Soviet-American Conference, held in Yalta, I interpreted for a few days."

"What sort of homecoming was it?" I asked.

"There was no homecoming," he said, with a laugh. "I just felt incarcerated. I belong right here. I couldn't wait to get out of Eastern Europe. As soon as I reached France, I picked up back issues of the Paris edition of the New York *Times*, and I read them all the way back across the Atlantic."

A few days later, on an unusually bright and sunny winter morning, I walked through the grounds of the U.N. to the Secretariat Building and met Sherry in the Press Club, on the third floor. The club was warm and pleasant, and Sherry's spirits were high. At the counter, he ordered "a bloody cow and black water," and interpreted this for me as a roast-beef sandwich and black coffee. When we had settled down at a table, he told me a little about the history of simultaneous interpretation. The League of Nations had only two official languages,

English and French, but, even so, its system of consecutive interpretation was time-consuming. A speech in German had to be followed by English and French versions, and while this gave the League delegates a chance to think, and to discuss what had been said, the method was never really satisfactory. At some small meetings, therefore, if everyone was familiar with, say, French, interpretation was dispensed with. The League's International Labor Organization, for instance, often conducted its meetings entirely in French. These were sometimes attended by Edward Filene, of Boston, a philanthropist who worked actively for peace and the cause of labor, and since he knew little French, he used to have a friend whisper to him in English about what was going on. It was the Bostonian's ignorance of French that ultimately led to simultaneous interpretation; after a meeting at which his friend was obliged to leave his elbow, Filene determined to discover a mechanical surrogate—a resolution that was later put into effect, with the help of the philanthropist's money, by A. G. Finlay, an engineer. Finlay developed a headphone system whereby a speech could be simultaneously translated into six languages and any one of the six could be piped straight to the ears of the headphone's user. Filene's electrical friend was first used at Geneva in 1931 at a League of Nations Assembly. Later, it was further developed and improved by I.B.M. engineers. The machine proved its speed and usefulness at the Nuremberg trials (Göring complained that the new method had cut short his remaining life by three-fourths), and today, with some refinements, it is used in all the meeting rooms of the United Nations, including the Security Council Chamber; there, however, because the issues discussed are considered so sensitive, the consecutive method is also used, in English and French, to give the delegates, as in the League, time to think.

"Before simultaneous interpretation was adopted, it met with a lot of opposition in the U.N., especially from interpreters like the late André Kaminker, who never believed that sentence-by-sentence interpretation would work," Sherry concluded. "I mention Kaminker because he was the greatest of the consecutive interpreters. He felt that the interpreter's speech should be as artistic and as much an organic whole as that of the delegate. While listening to his delegate, Kaminker never took a note; he just stared at the speaker, and when the speech was finished—and sometimes it went on for an hour or two—Kaminker rose to his feet and delivered an oration that was very often better than the original. Now and again, the speaker whom Kaminker was interpreting would come up afterward and say, '*M. Kaminker, ce n'est pas ce que j'ai dit.*' '*Monsieur le Délégué,*' he would answer, with a shrug, '*c'est ce que vous eussiez dû dire.*'"

That afternoon, I went over to the General Assembly Building to observe Sherry in the act of doing some interpreting on the question of seating Communist China. I arrived at the English booth through a labyrinth of hallways and back stairs, to find Sherry already there. He was chatting with his boothmate, Theodore Fagan, a British-Argentine in his early forties with glasses and close-cropped hair, who was puffing furiously at a cigarette. The cubicle itself, high on one side of the auditorium, was not much larger than a couple of good-sized telephone booths, and it contained only three chairs and a built-in desk below a glass wall. On the desk was a long, neat boxlike object, containing electronic equipment and sprouting language selectors, microphones, earphones, and volume controls. We seated ourselves in the chairs and clamped on the earphones. Thirty feet below us were the blue-and-green hall and the delegations, with the aristocratic, cocker-spaniel head of the Assembly's president, Mongi Slim, unmistakable among them. Sherry explained that he interpreted all the Russian speeches and Fagan all the Spanish and that the two of them took turns interpreting the French. If there should be an unexpected Russian interpolation in the debate while Sherry was away from the booth, Fagan, who knows no Russian, would switch his selector to the Spanish or French version of the Russian speech and interpret—or, technically, relay—from it. The Nationalist Chinese, happily, always spoke in English.

"The great triumph of Georgie-Porgie," Fagan said, his hand nervously playing with the microphone switch, "was when he translated Vishinsky's allusion to Pushkin's 'Boris Godunov' by a quote from 'Macbeth.' A great virtuoso, my boothmate, a great virtuoso."

"It was *noth*ing," Sherry said earnestly. "You see, around 1950 there was guerrilla fighting between Greece, on the one hand, and Bulgaria and Albania, on the other. Vishinsky, while making a speech on the subject, shouted, 'The boys'—of the West, that is—'have bloodied themselves in front of our very eyes, and can say, in the words of the poet, "*I mal'chiki krovavye v glazakh!*"' I remembered the complete verse of Pushkin, so I naturally recognized this as an allusion to Boris's being haunted by the vision of Ivan the Terrible's sons, whom he had done to death so that he himself could sit on the throne. Nevertheless, I knew I was in the middle of a split-second linguistic crisis—you have one of them every ten minutes with a good speaker who knows his literature and has a fondness for metaphor. What flashed before my eyes was the face of Richard III, whose life paralleled that of Boris, but the words that rolled instantly off my tongue belonged to Macbeth. I found myself shouting into the microphone:

> Will all great Neptune's ocean wash this blood
> Clean from my hands? No, this my hand will rather
> The multitudinous sea incarnadine . . ."

In the soundproof booth, Sherry's voice had an unnatural muffled quality as he declaimed these lines, but it resumed its ordinary tone as he turned suddenly to his colleague and said, "Fagan, leave that switch alone. Otherwise, we'll be on the air."

"*You'll* be on the air," Fagan retorted. "*Who* forgot to turn off the microphone that time and *who* serenaded the burning ears of all the delegates with '*Pace e gioia*'?" Fagan's wooden voice rose in a clumsy rendition of the aria:

> "*Pace e gioia,*
> *Basta, basta,*
> *Basta per pietà—*"

"*Avant de donner la parole au premier orateur inscrit* . . ." I heard through the earphones, obliterating the vague Assembly crowd noises of a second before.

Fagan's *"Pace e gioia"* instantly ceased, and before I knew what was happening, Sherry's hand had flicked the switch, and his twangy voice, snapped to attention, was saying firmly into the microphone, "Before I call on the first speaker on my list . . ." Meanwhile, the French words were spilling into my earphones in a rush: ". . . *je tiens à rappeler aux Membres de l'Assemblée que la liste des orateurs sur les deux points que nous examinons actuellement sera close cet après-midi à six heures."* It was only when, an instant afterward, I heard "6 P.M." in English that I realized that Sherry had kept pace, and that I had unconsciously taken in his English translation ("I should like to remind members of the Assembly that the list of speakers for the two items now being discussed will be closed at 6 P.M.") from outside the earphones.

This pronouncement was followed immediately by a Ghanaian delegate's speech, which, being in English, gave us a breathing space. I complimented Sherry on his instantaneous response.

"Oh, it means nothing," he said, dismissing it with a wave of the hand. "I find that subliminally I am listening through the earphones all the time, and somewhere, in some layer of my memory, it's all registered—including, for example, what the Ghanaian delegate is saying this second. Just let a single foreign word intrude into his speech and my hand will fly out to the switch and I'll be in action." ·

"Do you ever come to know the delegates you interpret?" I asked.

Sherry shook his head.

Fagan said, "Yes, occasionally, but some of them I

wouldn't want to know, and in any case the U.N. is too large now for interpreters to be included in cocktail parties."

"It's part of our job to be unobtrusive and anonymous," Sherry said. "To be only voices."

"There is no future in the job," Fagan said. "Except that now and then you do get to know the mind of a delegate. All interpreters are normally assigned to particular committees, and they usually come to plenary Assembly meetings like this one only when a question that concerns their committee is being discussed. George and I are both attached to the Political Committee, and we find that after you've interpreted a delegate on China or the Congo you overflow with information on his point of view—to such an extent that if in the heat of debate he makes a slip, you automatically correct it in—"

Sherry flicked a switch and started interpreting the second speaker on the list—L. F. Palarmarchuk, of the Ukraine. I turned my selector to the Russian, to catch the sound of Mr. Palarmarchuk's voice; it was thin and boyish. I returned to the English, and heard Sherry's firm, twangy voice talking in the earphones and also in the booth, in a weird echo. "The point is, of course," it was saying belligerently, "that, while adopting the slogan 'Make haste slowly,' the Western Powers intend, as before, to sidestep the solution of a perfectly clear and fully ripe question and to continue their cowardly policy of moratorium with regard to the restoration of China's legitimate rights in the United Nations. We do not consider that the position of the ostrich, which hides its head in the sand, is an intelligent position. The majority of sound-thinking people throughout the world are openly deriding this ostrich policy, which considers that the world will stop changing once the ostrich has closed its eyes. We are surprised that responsible representatives of the United States government consider the ostrich's position to be the acme of wise statesmanship—so much so that they even boast about and preen themselves on the game of the moratorium which they thought up. . . ."

A few days later, I stopped in at the Secretariat around ten o'clock in the morning to call on Sherry again, and found him unenthusiastically waiting to interpret the Security Council's ceremonial recommendation of the General Assembly's admission of the U.N.'s hundred-and-fourth member, Tanganyika. "No fireworks this morning," he said as we made our way from the Secretariat lobby to the Security Council's English booth. "Without exception, everyone will congratulate Tanganyika, and the whole debate will be as dull as ditchwater. Smooth sailing is fine, but a good hand would much rather sail in rough waters."

Inside the booth, Sherry introduced me to two colleagues—Nicholas Spoov, a tall, thin man with a small face and baby-blue eyes, whom Sherry described as "originally a Shanghai Russian, now a naturalized Canadian, with an engineering degree from McGill," and Richard Ross, a rather solemn-looking American. Then Sherry went out into the chamber, where he was to do some consecutive interpreting, à la Kaminker. Ross and

Spoov started discussing the morning's speakers. Our booth was beside and above a large horseshoe table, around which were ranged the eleven delegates, with Omar Loutfi, of the United Arab Republic, who was the president for the month, at the apex of the horseshoe. Bisecting the horseshoe was an oblong table, at which were seated four interpreters—two for English and two for French—and several verbatim reporters and press officers. The most prominent thing in the room was a towering and somewhat grotesque mural behind the president, which told the story of man's progression from the darkness of ignorance into the light of technology; the slain dragon and the prisoners behind bars were done in gloomy gray, green, and black, the brighter colors being reserved for celebrants, flowers, machines, and microscopes.

On my left, the rather dry voice of Ross started racing with the president's French: "Before proceeding to the agenda, I should like to express to Ambassador Zorin, the representative of the Soviet Union, on behalf of the members of the Security Council, our gratitude for the manner in which he conducted the debates of the Security Council during the course of his tenure of office as president of the Council. . . ."

After the president's remarks had been translated consecutively into English, Spoov, on my right, skipped through Zorin's reply: "Mr. President, I wish to thank you most sincerely for the thanks that you have addressed to me, and in turn I should like to express the wish that you will be successful in carrying out the responsible tasks of the presidency. . . ."

Sir Patrick Dean, of the United Kingdom, and Nathan Barnes, of Liberia, made their formal speeches in English, with floor interpreters supplying interstitial French versions. Then came Professor Gunapala Piyasena Malalasekera, of Ceylon, who talked with more emotion about the Tanganyikans. "Tanganyika is a country unique in many ways," Malalasekera said. "Archeologists say that it may well have been the cradle of the human race. The Olduvai skull of what has been called the 'Nutcracker Man,' which was found there, belongs to the oldest human being at present known to science, and has been ascribed to an age between one and two million years, doubling thereby the accepted antiquity of mankind." Armand Bérard, of France, who followed Malalasekera, spoke in exquisite French, which Spoov nimbly translated from the booth. But the heartfelt words of the Ceylonese had evidently caught the attention of Adlai Stevenson, who seemed to have as lively a pair of ears as the interpreters, and hardly less of a penchant for improvisation. When Bérard and his interpreter had finished speaking, Stevenson took the floor. "If American slang is not forbidden," he said, "I could express the hope that the United Nations might find in Tanganyika another 'Nutcracker Man.'" Everyone in the Council turned to look at Prime Minister Julius Nyerere, who had flown from Tanganyika specially to attend the meeting, but Spoov merely said, "How do you suppose one would make the Stevenson pun in French?"

I said I didn't know.

Spoov waited eagerly for the consecutive man to re-run the "Nutcracker" sentence. *"Si l'on me permet de m'exprimer dans le langage familier américain,"* the floor interpreter soon said sonorously in the earphones, *"je formule l'espoir que les Nations Unies trouveront au Tanganyika un autre homme 'casse-noisette.'* "

"It's not quite right," Spoov said in a discouraged tone. "Not quite right."

Between Stevenson and Zorin, who was to speak last, there were several routine speeches of welcome, and except when Ross was running the Spanish course, Spoov talked with some animation about various Sherry interpretational feats. "Once," he recalled, "when the delegate from the Soviet Union was taking to task the speakers who had preceded him by referring to them all as 'honorable delegates,' Sherry, with a bow to Shakespeare's Antony, interpolated, 'So are they all, all honorable delegates.' And then there was the time when he came up against a Russian proverb. The Russian delegate was talking about all capitalistic countries' having a natural attraction for each other, and said, *'Kulik kulika vidit izdaleka.'* George knew that *'kulik'* was some sort of swamp bird, but, as he later remarked, he'd never learned the names of all the birds, because 'the whole lot of them refused to talk back to me.' Anyway, being unable to think of a literal translation for the exact bird, he came up with a similar English proverb, 'Birds of a feather flock together.' "

"That's not the best one," Ross said slowly, putting down his earphones. (The Nationalist Chinese had the floor, and many people were openly not listening.) "Do you remember the time Sherry was interpreting that

French delegate, and the honorable delegate said very prosaically, in French, that the resolution about Cuba had been amended beyond recognition, though the spirit still remained? Sherry's translation was 'The resolution is like a Cheshire cat, which has gradually disappeared, leaving only the grin.' "

There was a stir in the chamber. Nationalist China had finished, and Russia was about to speak. Spoov, who had turned several of Khrushchev's anti-colonialist speeches into English in 1960, now interpreted Zorin's homily, which seemed to me remarkable only for its lack of rhetorical flourishes. All during Zorin's speech, Sherry sat chin in hand and stared at Zorin. He took only a few notes. "That was short and sweet," Spoov said at the end of the simultaneous, and then, as Sherry began to speak, he listened to find out whether Sherry, in the consecutive, would improve on his rendering. Like Kaminker before him, Sherry seemed to be redelivering the speech word for word.

I asked Spoov how Sherry did it.

"When a speech is being made, Sherry jots down the key words—the operative words—of the sentences," Spoov said. "For instance, if Zorin says, 'In the Congo, mercenaries are a hideous manifestation of the age-old, eternal iron heel of imperialism,' Sherry is likely to jot down 'hideous' and 'mercenary.' But I am really as mystified as you are."

As the Maestro concluded his tour de force, Spoov shook his head in wonderment.

1962

1971. In 1962, George Sherry left interpreting to become a senior officer in the Office of the Under-Secretaries-General for Special Political Affairs, a position he still holds. During this period, he has been on mission assignments to Elisabethville (1962–63), Leopoldville (1964), Cyprus (1964–65), and Lahore (1965–66).

II

The Third

IN MANY COUNTRIES, RADIO HAS LOST GROUND
to television and the report of the eye, and has ceased to
be a creative force. In England, however, the British
Broadcasting Corporation, which has a monopoly on
broadcast sound and transmits four domestic services—the
Light Programme, the Home Programme, the Third
Programme, and a recent addition called Network
Three—continues to enjoy a prestige akin to that of
Parliament and the British courts of law. In fact, the
B.B.C. remains the peerless patron of the arts in the British
Isles. It employs one out of every five symphony musicians; substantially contributes to the economies of the
opera houses, the music festivals, and the great orches-
tras; and is the greatest source of poetry copyright pay-
ments (a half hour of reading on the B.B.C. can often
earn more for a poet than the book from which he
reads). Moreover, intellectual sound has been experienc-
ing a sort of renaissance in Britain since the war. A
B.B.C. official recently gave several reasons for it. "For
one thing, sound is cheaper than vision," he explained.
"To mount a play on television costs us six times what it
costs to produce it on wireless. For another thing, be-

cause we are a monopoly, we can sometimes afford to produce a program with a listening population of no more than ten thousand. Then, too, while in the theatre a writer is at the mercy of the backers—many of whom are concerned only with commercial success—with us, once an idea for a broadcast is approved, the writer, the producer, and the actors have complete freedom. But, most important of all, sound has inherent advantages over vision in reproducing literature. To create mood, time, and space, both writing and radio rely on words and imagination. Television, on the other hand, depends on the cumbersome and limiting apparatus of cameras and sets. It is especially crippled in dealing with modern writing, which is often made up of interior monologue and half-real dream sequences. Say a Joyce wants to portray a dazed man walking through the Dublin streets. On television, each person or object on the way has to be shown; on radio and in literature, they can be evoked."

The advantages of sound have nowhere been better understood or utilized than on the Third Programme, which has a budget of about a million pounds a year and at present broadcasts, roughly, from eight to eleven o'clock on weekday evenings, and two or three hours longer on weekends. (Since the Third's maiden broadcast, on September 29, 1946, the service has been emulated in West Germany, Italy, and Belgium. In the United States, however, even placing the Third's recorded broadcasts has proved a problem, although they are available to any station for little more than the cost of the postage.) The Third broadcasts some of the best talks heard on the radio anywhere, and, in music, mounts original productions and full-length operas, and explores the lifetime works of past and present composers, including some who have been forgotten altogether and others who have never been heard in modern times. In drama, it airs the entire repertoires of important authors; performs classics of many periods and countries (some in translation, others in the original language); produces plays by contemporary dramatists from Spain, Egypt, and most points between; serializes most major novels capable of adaptation; and presents portraits of eminent people, imaginary conversations, and parodies. (Portraits are better suited to radio than to television, since the mosaics assembled from the tape recorder do not overwhelm the subject with the personalities of those recalling him.)

From the first day of the Third's broadcasts, the program has nourished the hopes of intellectuals. At its inception, the writer Edward Sackville-West noted, "The Third Programme may well become the greatest educative and civilizing force England has known since the secularization of the theatre in the sixteenth century." The composer Ralph Vaughan Williams later called its broadcasts "perhaps the greatest musical event that has happened in this country . . . at once the envy and the admiration of all," while T. S. Eliot was no less fervent in his praise, if a little less direct, when he said, "I think that there must be many people in this country to whom the Third Programme is important because they are isolated and do not know how to inform themselves; because their education has been inadequate and they wish to supply its deficiencies; or because opportunities for hearing the best music, seeing the best drama, and listening to the highest authorities on various subjects are not otherwise available to them."

The Third is the creation of one man, Sir William John Haley, who today, at the age of sixty-one, sits in the editor's chair at the London *Times*—for him, the apex of the journalistic profession. Even though Haley has altogether left broadcasting for newspaper journalism, he continues to be the Third's main inspiration. Haley is a medium-sized man with sharp blue eyes, whose face, even to its look of abstracted diffidence, recalls that of the late Dag Hammarskjöld. Appropriately, the father of "the greatest educative force" has spent most of his life in search of education, and whenever he has not been making money for his employers he has been giving himself a university education through his reading. He has never been able to take culture for granted. It has always been something to be chased, mastered, and guarded—perhaps because he had to work to overcome social and economic handicaps almost from birth.

Less is known about the early life of Haley than about that of practically any other public figure in England. A wish for anonymity and an impenetrable shyness have made his origins even more obscure, and his becoming the editor of the *Times*, in 1952, did not help matters. As far as can be made out, William John Haley was born in St. Helier, on the island of Jersey. When he was two, he lost his father, Frank Haley, a clerk from Yorkshire. The death deprived the boy of a stable home and eventually led him to seek refuge in reading. His mother, a French greengrocer's daughter, née Marie Sangan, remarried. Her second husband's name is not known, but he appears to have been a good stepfather. He had spent some time in Australia, and by telling William stories of his exploits there he stimulated the child's love of adventure. He also put William into the best secondary school on the island, Victoria College, where he was fortunate in having two helpful teachers—a former headmaster of another school and a retired actor who taught Shakespeare's plays by speaking all the parts. When William was sixteen (it was the third year of the First World War), he was out of school and was working as a wireless operator on a tramp steamer. By following a great-books course, he continued his education at sea, where he remained for nearly two years—until the captain of the ship assembled all hands aft and announced, "The war's over. That's the end of your danger money." William returned to Jersey and applied for a job with one of the South American branches of Harrods, the London store. While waiting for an answer, he chanced to meet on the street the editor of the Jersey *Morning News*; this man, knowing the boy's interest in books, launched him on his profession by letting him write articles for the paper. When, after a time, William asked for pay, he was silenced with half a crown a week. He sweated it out for a year, keeping up with his reading, and managing to acquire shorthand and German on the side; he knew French already. Then, still under twenty, he moved to London to improve his position. He was hired by the *Times* as a telephonist—the work amounted to copying down in shorthand the dispatches phoned in by the paper's Continental staff—and it was from this tenuous position that he built his career. He suggested that all the European telephone calls be routed through the Brussels exchange, to save money. The *Times* adopted his scheme and sent him to Brussels to manage it, and in some cases it cut the costs of the Continental copy from half a crown a word to a penny. But the job, Haley was quick to recognize, was without a future (by now he had married Edith Gibbons, the secretary of the *Times'* foreign editor), and he began contributing weekly articles to the Manchester *Evening News*. He was drawn to it both because he was a natural liberal and because it was a back door to the much more intellectual Manchester *Guardian*. (The two papers had the same management, but the *News* had three times the circulation of the *Guardian*.) The articles did credit to Haley's self-education; the managing editor of the *News*, when he met his writer for the first time, was taken aback by his youth. He nevertheless hired William as a staff reporter, and the Haleys moved to the North. Haley, too shy to be a good correspondent, found his niche in editing, but his advancements, which were quick and many, were due to financial acumen. First, when he was still in his twenties, he became the managing editor of the paper, with a seat on the board of governors; then he was made a director of the *Guardian-Evening News* corporation; and in 1939 he began sharing the managing directorship of the two papers with the wise, liberal ruler of the *Guardian*, John Scott. In Manchester, Haley made his mark not by setting editorial policy (he was mostly on the business side), and not by scoring social or intellectual successes (he never went to a pub or a club; instead, in solitude, he drank milk late into the night and pored over books), but by hard work (his only relaxation seems to have been playing table tennis in the paper's canteen with anyone on the staff), by a little ruthlessness (idle men were shown the door), by a concern for popular education (he always wrote the weekly book reviews himself), and, most of all, by an unblinking attention to news and to solvency.

From Manchester, Haley moved to London, where his businesslike touch saved first Reuters, the news agency, and then the B.B.C. One of the sources of the B.B.C.'s strength when it was founded, in 1922, was its broadcasting monopoly, which enabled it to set its sights high—sometimes over the heads of its listeners. But since the departure of its first and powerful director-general, Lord Reith, in 1938, the Corporation had begun to flounder. Under Reith's successors—first Sir Frederick Ogilvie, a don, and then Robert William Foot and Captain Sir Cecil Graves, who jointly tried to fill Reith's chair, only to give currency to the quip "The B.B.C. has a Foot in the Grave"—financial troubles threatened its independence. Haley, who arrived at the B.B.C. in 1943, quickly restored it to solvency, and within a year he was rewarded with its director-generalship. At last, the poor boy from the provinces had moved from a preoccupation with finance to the possibilities of culture, and had thereupon become one of the most influential leaders of the arts in Britain. "As guardian of our national forum, newspaper, theatre, opera, schoolroom, and lecture hall of the air," the *Observer* commented later, "he is the less likely to compromise the freedom, or lower the quality, of this complex institution just because his values are self-chosen, and because he is as immune to intimidation as a lighthouse keeper."

At that time, the B.B.C. had two categories of program on the air—an all-purpose radio entertainment called the Home, and a lighter broadcast, suitable for groups in canteens, barracks, and dugouts at home and overseas, known as the Forces Programme. Haley was shocked to find that neither had ever broadcast items like the uncut version of "Hamlet" and "The Ring of the Nibelung." When he asked "Why not?" he was told that such intellectual wares were too eccentric, too long, and too demanding for broadcasting. They called for sustained listening, when what the radio public required was a staple of regulars—the same daily or weekly entertainment programs, news reports, and weather forecasts. The "Hamlet"s and the "Ring"s, when broadcast at all, had to be chiselled down and wedged between "fixed points." It was maintained that people never made provision for listening, in the way that theatregoers planned an evening out; they listened from habit. A bell went off in their heads at the time of "The Goon Show," the news broadcasts, or the "Woman's Hour," and they automatically flicked on the set. The only hope of leading the public out of the cave of easy continuous listening and entertainment, it was thought, lay in a gradual stiffening of the drink of boogie-woogie and "The Goon Show" with Bach and "Beowulf." To Haley, this seemed an "education by stealth," and also one without a realizable end in sight. Moreover, he became convinced that his predecessors and the nine B.B.C. governors, to whom the director-general answered, had been pursuing a contradictory aim: on the one hand, they had been giving the listener what he wanted, and, on the other, they had been trying dutifully to elevate his taste and intelligence. As far as Haley was concerned, the outcome of this policy was a Gadarene slope of compromise—a point of view shared by the historian and critic Harold Nicolson, who was one of the governors at the time. Nicolson later wrote, "We all tended to view our problems [of double duty] from each angle simultaneously; our vision thus became bifocal. . . . If the listening public could in fact be sharply divided between the long-distance and the short-distance, the bifocal system would work well enough. [But] the gradations between the highly cultivated, the averagely cultivated, and the uncultivated are as numerous and as imprecise as those of the spectroscope. Our attempts to strike a happy medium between the long-distance and the short-distance led us to concentrate our attention on the line of contact between them; the result was a blur. . . . An oily, unctuous coating of compromise descended upon the presentation of the more difficult items; we became aware that in seeking, from the best of motives, to popularize culture, we were offending against its dignity, degrading its essential values, and not attaining those standards of perfection at which so great an institution should surely aim." Nicolson went on to illustrate the compromise: "I strove for long to obtain a short period for poetry reading; in the end, I obtained my desire; but when I opened the *Radio Times*, I found that this unpalatable item had been tendered to the listener under the matey title 'V. for Verse.' In response to my enraged protests, this title was subsequently altered. But the incident was for me instructive. . . . It convinced me that something must be wrong if the British public (inheritors of the greatest literature that the world has ever known) must have their poetry presented to them as if it were castor-oil in a spoon."

Haley set himself the task of rescuing British culture from the medicinal spoon, resolving that a new wave length that would become available to the B.B.C. at the conclusion of the war should be reserved exclusively for a cultural program. He envisioned the program as rising like a phoenix from the ashes of all the conventions of broadcasting. The first such convention was the strait jacket of fixed points. Haley vowed that his program would have "blank days, blank weeks, blank years" in which to explore a topic or a composition at as great a length or to as great a depth as was deemed necessary; the works of fifty Victorian poets in fifty lectures would not be considered too long, and operas, plays, and speeches would be allowed to run their course without interruptions for news, weather forecasts, or even station breaks. The second convention concerned listening from habit. On the new wave length, it was to be taken for granted that listeners would arrange to be beside their radios just as they arranged to be in their theatre seats. Listeners, like theatregoers, would be kept posted on the offerings by notices in the press. Finally, the old idea that material once used was dead was to be discarded in favor of the view that a good program could bear a second and third listening; in any case, listeners would need at least two or three repeat broadcasts, since their lives could hardly be built entirely around the radio set. Repeats would be routine. In this way, Haley hoped to put the treasures of all nations within the reach of everyone who could afford a set but not attendance at a university in London or a theatre in Paris. So preoccupied was he with the freedom of his program from established rules that he balked at giving it a name at all, thinking that this might have the effect of predetermining, however slightly, its nature. After much soul-searching, he settled on what he took to be a neutral title—the Third Programme—but by now "Third" is as much of a shibboleth, and has acquired as many connotations, as "highbrow" or "egghead."

In 1944, after some altercation with his subordinates, Haley set forth his vision in writing and went before his governors. His proposal was received by most of them with skeptical bleats. Governor Nicolson has recorded one typical exchange: "If the Third Programme were to live up to such ambitious motives, might it not often become dull? 'Yes,' [Haley] answered, 'let it often become dull. Let it often make mistakes. . . . Let it arouse controversy, and not seek to muffle controversy. . . . Let it set a standard, and furnish an example, which will not only raise the level of our own broadcasting but in the end affect the level of broadcasting in other lands.' " And what was to happen to the two existing programs? Haley replied that they would be beamed to different areas of the public brow. The Light—the successor to the Forces Programme—would concentrate on the lower part of the forehead, with "The Goon Show," plus such tantalizing treats as an act of "The Waltz of the Toreadors" wedged in now and again to whet the mass appetite for culture. The Home would aim at the middle region of the forehead—*two* acts of "The Waltz of the Toreadors" and a stream of Beethoven symphonies. As for the Third, it would strike out for the crown of the head—all three acts of the "Toreadors" and the last Beethoven quartets. Some of the board members charged Haley with a snobbish, "three-tier" view of culture, but his proposal received acclaim from two quarters—from Nicolson and from Lady Violet Bonham Carter (another governor and the daughter of a former Prime Minister), of whom it has been said that "to argue with her is like fighting a tank with a perambulator." Moreover, Haley, as director-general, was a sort of dictator, and it was not long before, in the words of Lady Violet, "the Forces of Light vanquished the Forces of Darkness." The new program was assigned six hours an evening, from six o'clock to midnight, and it now awaited only the end of hostilities and the installation of some of the best available transmitters to take to the British airwaves.

Haley's choice for the first head—or controller, as he is called—of the Third was the late Sir George Barnes. Barnes, in his two-year stewardship, from 1946 to 1948, made the program the exclusive domain of the élite, an adjunct of Oxford and Cambridge. He had come to the wider world of the B.B.C. from the genteel atmosphere of King's College, Cambridge, and from the cozy house of the Cambridge University Press, where he had developed a lasting interest in the aesthetic side of publishing. He once said to Harman Grisewood, an Oxford man, who was his assistant and ultimately succeeded him as controller, "You Oxford men are the worldly men. You are the heirs of Benjamin Jowett. You all want to be Prime Ministers. You will all end up in the corridors of power. We Cambridge men are without ambitions. We want only to think and read quietly, to live our lives in retreats, by the candles of the eternal verities." Under Barnes, the Third talked less to the isolated Haleys in English hamlets than to the scholars watching over the British Museum, but if the director-general had any doubts about Barnes' choice of an audience, he did not voice them. Indeed, when television erupted in England, Haley persuaded Barnes to manage it, hoping to nurse the pariah of mass communication along in the shadow of the Third. Barnes stayed on the job for six years, but when he was offered the position of principal of a new university at Keele, in North Staffordshire, he cheerfully left the B.B.C.; at least, Keele was in the same milieu as the Third. How much he was part of that world, and it of him, emerges clearly in Haley's commemorative words at Barnes' death, in 1960: "Even as an undergraduate, he was imbued with Plato's idea of Guardians. The idea grew as his circle widened. . . . And if Barnes . . . spoke of such things with a smile and was never far from teasing, that was because his care for both principles and people was gentle as well as strong. He might seek to guard the Guardians, but he knew it could be done only through patience and love. . . . Once, in his home here at Keele, he played me something on the piano and spoke of the unease I ought to feel until the music returned to its original key. It was in search of his original key that Sir George Barnes came to the University College of North Staffordshire."

As controller, Grisewood followed Barnes' example. The Platonist regime lasted six years altogether, but before the end of Grisewood's term the seismograph in the Third offices had started to register tremors. The staffs of the other B.B.C. services increasingly complained that the Third was siphoning away the best material. Also, the vision of the Third as a cultural lift had proved a mirage; those who could sup at the table of David merely by turning a knob were slothfully continuing to feast with the Goliaths of Light and Home. Out of a listening population of thirty-three million, an average Third broadcast drew no more than a hundred thousand. Furthermore, the new venture was being assailed in the press. Cassandra, of the *Daily Mirror*, the most popular columnist in England, charged that the Third "has degenerated into an ineffectual freak, influencing those who organize it, those who perform on it, and precious few else," and added, "The drum of culture has rarely been beaten with such expensive feathers in so high a vacuum." The *Evening Standard* felt that the program, instead of aiming its beams at readers in the public library, pointed them at "Bloomsbury and its greenery-yallery, Grosvenor Gallery, 'Foot-in-the-Grave young men.'" The *Daily Sketch* was a bit more specific in its choice of a target: "From the Third Programme of the B.B.C. last night came a tumbling stream of words. It was . . . George Barker's 'True Confession.' . . . Had any newspaper dared to print such gilded filth, a storm of protest would have followed. The Lord Chamberlain would never have permitted this on the stage of a public theatre, or the Board of Film Censors on a screen. . . . The Third Programme is a public voice and a public entertainment. Where are its censors?" The better papers and periodicals—the *Observer*, the *Spectator*, the *New Statesman*—went for the same Achilles' heel, though in a more gingerly way, the *New Statesman* calling the program "a Barmecide feast," and also describing it as

> . . . striving to surpass
> Samson, who, with the jawbone of an ass,
> Only laid low a thousand Philistines.

Between 1952 and 1958, when John Morris, another King's man and a longtime writer about the East and the Gurkhas, held the controllership, there was a failure of nerve within the inner chambers of the Third. (At least some of the despair could be traced to the postwar proliferation of B.B.C. television—it opened an escape hatch from the Corporation's sound monopoly, which had made the Third possible in the first place. Then, in 1954, the introduction of commercial television struck another blow at Haley's idea of using the complete planning power provided by monopoly to elevate public taste.) The man who might have stood up to the critics had left the B.B.C. in 1952 for the *Times*. The director-general's chair was now occupied by an Army professional, Lieutenant-General Sir Ian Jacob. Where Haley had always tried to lift the standards of broadcasting, it was understood that Jacob intended to put some of the Third into

Home, put some of the Home into Light, and, by popularizing sound, keep the listeners devoted to radio despite the growing temptations of television. Early in 1957, Jacob announced his plans for a reorganization of the Third. Its broadcast time was to be cut from five or six hours to three. A "wider provision for the minority interest" was to be made, by turning over to a new Network Three the time that the Third had lost. Network Three was conceived of as a cafeteria school for foreign-language enthusiasts, bridge players, pigeon fanciers, and stamp collectors—a sort of dog's breakfast. In the future, the B.B.C. would put greater emphasis on relaxation, variety, and entertainment.

The Third's supporters formed committees, held press conferences, inspired editorials, and sent off a barrage of letters to the newspapers. One such letter, printed in the *Times* and signed by Lord Beveridge, Arthur Bliss, Adrian Boult, the Bishop of Chichester, T. S. Eliot, E. M. Forster, Christopher Fry, John Gielgud, Victor Gollancz, John Masefield, Harold Nicolson, Bertrand Russell, V. Sackville-West, Ralph Vaughan Williams, and Peter Laslett, carried intellectual authority, although the *Daily Mirror* termed the signatories "fifteen Third Programme fans [who] include . . . a Peer of seventy-eight, another Peer of eighty-four, a poet getting on for seventy, a composer of eighty-four, a writer in his seventies, a bishop of seventy-four." Next, spokesmen of the international community of letters rallied behind the "fans" in an epistle signed by Albert Camus, Jean Cocteau, Bertrand de Jouvenel, André Malraux, André Maurois, Gabriel Marcel, Darius Milhaud, Jacques Maritain, Richard Rovere, and Lionel Trilling. At last, in July, a deputation was allowed to wait on the governors of the B.B.C. Michael Tippett and Ralph Vaughan Williams put the case for musicians, and Sir Laurence Olivier that for actors, but the most stinging harangue came from Eliot, who spoke in behalf of the talkers and poets: "I . . . allowed myself [at first] to be persuaded by the official assurance that the shorter time would mean a better Third Programme. But two hours a day is seven hundred and thirty hours a year, and this *could* mean that two thousand one hundred and ninety less talks were broadcast each year. Even when the proportions are balanced out between drama, music, and the spoken word, it is clear that that innocuous little two hours in fact represents a catastrophic blow to the entire Third Programme, and it is likely that the spoken word will be among the heavier sufferers. . . . This [new plan] seems to me a plan to pander to the more moronic elements in our society, and to drive the minority further into its corner at a time when, as never before, there is an opportunity to increase the numbers of the minority. The day of bread and circuses is over; the general culture level of the community is rising; the B.B.C. should provide more and more leaven." But all the eloquent representations made no impression on the authorities; on October 1, 1957, the amputated program went on the air. (The era beyond bread and circuses was thrown a small piece of meat—two additional hours of Third on Saturdays—but not until a year later, as though to make it quite clear that this move was not due to public pressure.) If there was any consolation for the Third's supporters, it lay in the succession of Hugh Carleton Greene—a journalist brother of Graham Greene—to Jacob's chair in 1960, and in their belief that they had blunted the Philistine axe so that it would never be used again to chop away time from the Third.

Recently, a visitor stopped in at Broadcasting House, the B.B.C.'s headquarters in the West End of London—a building that resembles a ship, with windows like portholes. He made his way along many corridors to the few small rooms where the entire Third staff, of seven, plans its programs. He was received by P. H. Newby, who in 1958, at the age of forty, was appointed the fourth controller. Unlike his three predecessors, Newby is more or less a self-educated, self-made man; like Haley, he discovered culture on his own. (Newby's father was a baker in a small English village, and Newby himself has never taken a university degree.) He spent many years out of England, some of them in Egypt, the setting for his many novels, which have won him considerable literary acclaim. He is a quiet, unworldly, rather sphinxlike man, with a large head and a tightly drawn mouth, which give him a cerebral look. At first, his eyes appeared as inexpressive as the walls of his office (gray) and its furniture (modern), but as he talked on into the afternoon about the Third, he began radiating good cheer, though his voice maintained the neutral quality of a formal broadcast.

"With time, the cuts have become accepted as a fact of life," he said. "When I succeeded to this job, the first thing I did was to invite the research panel down to

Broadcasting House. This is a panel of a thousand volunteers, who listen to our programs and comment on them. It's like a reservoir with a tap at the top and a leak at the bottom; the water gets changed every two years. I thought the panel would be intimidated, so I prepared a story of my life: 'I am Newby. I was born in 1918. I spent some time at St. Paul's College, Cheltenham, and was in the Medical Corps during the war. I live in Buckinghamshire, twenty-five miles from London, with my wife and teen-age daughter. I am not a very social person. I get to the B.B.C. early in the morning, work here until late in the afternoon, listen to the Third in the evening at home, and fit my writing into weekends and into the time between work and listening to the Third.' But as soon as the panel arrived, I hardly had a chance to say anything. They went at each other, now talking about a play they didn't like, now about an opera they did like." Newby went on to explain that the editorial responsibility for the Third was shared, in a system of checks and balances. The departments of Talks, Music, Drama, and Features, each with its own head and its own stable of producers, offered programs and program ideas to the planners and the controller of the service, who held the purse strings. Newby said that he and his fellow-buyers depended heavily on the producers—the sellers—who thought up ideas for programs, scouted for talent, worked as independent agents and editors, and converted an idea into a finished broadcast. They were collectively as interesting a group of people as could be found anywhere; many of them were artists and musicians and writers of national repute.

Newby's assistant, Leslie Stokes, dropped in. In the course of talking about plans for the program, the two planners discussed the Third's producers. (In theory, any of the producers on the B.B.C. staff can do a program for the Third, but in practice most of them automatically sort themselves out into "eggheads," or Third producers, and "pompadours," or Light and Home producers.) The Talks producers for the Third included Miss Anna Kallin, a polyglot Russian émigré; T. S. Gregory, onetime president of the Aquinas Society; Miss Leonie Cohn, a specialist in art and architecture; George MacBeth, a young poet; and David Edge, who took his Ph.D. in radio astronomy. Drama for the Third came from Michael Bakewell, noted for his productions of Harold Pinter; Martin Esslin, the author of "The Theatre of the Absurd" and the successor to Donald McWhinnie, who is currently working as a director in the West End and on Broadway; Raymond Raikes, known for his productions of Greek, Elizabethan, and Jacobean plays; and Herman Fortuin, a Dutch satirist and playwright. But the greatest number of producers worked in the Features department, among them Douglas Cleverdon (he had recently made radio experiments in *musique concrète*), Christopher Sykes (he made Ivy Compton-Burnett novels speak on the radio), Louis MacNeice (he could turn anything into verse), Geoffrey Bridson (he was good at drawing out Ezra Pound or Pete Seeger in front of the microphone), and, finally, Rayner Heppenstall, who exercised his talents with bilingual programs devoted to French poetry and large-scale dramatic works, and Christopher Holme, who was most comfortable in making musicals out of good books. The situation in Music was "far more complicated," Stokes said. William Glock, whose musical taste had proved too avant-garde for the readers of the *Observer's* music column, which he had written for six years, had arrived at the B.B.C. in 1959 with a broom. He had swept aside the "fuddy-duddies" (supporters of Debussy and the Beethoven symphonies) in favor of the partisans of contemporary music (the music of Webern, Schoenberg, Berg, Boulez). The quantity of atonal, nerve-end music had gone up, to the dyspepsia of the older producers and the comfort of the younger ones.

"This seems like one of our weekly meetings," Stokes said at one point during the talk about the producers.

"Yes, the meetings *are* like a bazaar, aren't they?" Newby agreed. He explained that at the meetings the controllers and the producers talked in turn around the table, criticizing the programs already broadcast, arguing about new ideas, taking to task now this writer, now that actor or composer. During a Drama meeting, the buyers and sellers might try to think up a good play for a particular actor, or a particular play for a good actor; or a controversy about "Hamlet" might make them resolve on a new interpretation of the play; or Newby might suggest to the producers a play by an unknown author that he and the script department had liked; or they all might decide to repeat a program with a new cast or in a new translation.

Since 1960, the Thursday Invitation Concerts have been weekly Third offerings. They owe their existence to Glock, who has established a reputation among the critics for imaginative programming. (He may bill together, say, a Beethoven septet and a work by Oliver Messiaen, to make some indirect musical comparison.) He has used these concerts for exposing the ear to different categories of musical sound, for making a dramatic contrast between choral and orchestral works, and for introducing audiences to difficult masterpieces of the twentieth century. The concerts have made the B.B.C. the primary musical force in England, enlarged the small role of chamber music, and broadened the island outlook of British music to encompass the European experience.

A few miles from Broadcasting House, in one of the B.B.C.'s Maida Vale studios (the Corporation has fifty-nine studios in London), the excitement of one of these concerts was being generated at a rehearsal held on a spring day. The studio, which has dry acoustics, well suited to broadcasting, and is large enough to accommodate an audience of four hundred, invited each Thursday, was alive with the New Music Ensemble, led by a boyish conductor, John Carewe. The program consisted of Henze's Serenade for Solo Cello; Beethoven's Bagatelles; Webern's Two Songs and Four Songs (with Josephine Nendick, mezzo-soprano); John Field's Piano Sonata in C Minor; and Hindemith's Kammermusik No. 3 for Cello and Ten Solo Instruments. The stage was crowded with musicians (four strings, five woodwinds, three brasses, and a piano), microphones, and a cobweb of cables. A technician in a yellow jumper wove in and out among the wires, adjusting the direction of the microphones and aligning the orchestra members' chairs. The producer, Leo Black, who had auditioned and engaged the group, sat with another technician in a cubicle overlooking the studio. When the rehearsal got under way, he instructed the technician how to mix and balance the sounds, or called out to the conductor through a microphone for more cello, less violin. Meanwhile, on the platform, Carewe made his suggestions about interpretation to the players. The rehearsals of the Henze and Beethoven pieces went forward routinely into the early afternoon. The Webern songs, however, presented difficulties. Black and Carewe instructed Miss Nendick not to "swell" the notes, and to drain her voice of all emotion, explaining that the success of the songs depended on her ability to capture "the neurotic Austria of Freud, Berg, and Oskar Kokoschka." After a few tries, Miss Nendick was declared to have captured it.

In Broadcasting House itself, in Studio 8, Louis Mac-Neice was in the second day of rehearsing Goethe's "Faust." Some years earlier, he had written and produced a verse translation of the epic in six installments; now he had done a new, abbreviated version. The idea for a three-hour taped production of it had been approved, and for some days MacNeice had been hard at work casting it, and booking studios, engineers, and recording devices. Surrounded by engineers and a secretary, he was sitting in a booth in front of a row of switches and gazing intently through the glass wall that separated him from a roomful of actors and actresses. Nervous tension, scattered instruction sheets, sound-effects records, and an array of mechanical apparatus gave the room the atmosphere of the cockpit of an airplane at the moment of takeoff.

"Mephisto, can you drop your voice an octave or so?" MacNeice said over the intercom. "It should be deep."

"Like the blue sea, Louis?" came the voice of Mephistopheles, in bass tones. He got a ripple of unsure laughter from the cast.

"All right," MacNeice said. "Let's take the scene through again."

All concerned, on both sides of the glass partition, pencils in hand, turned to their scripts. A signal light went on, and a second later the studio was transformed into a cosmic stage by the contrapuntal voices of Mephistopheles, low and resonant, and Faust, high-pitched and distraught:

> "I like to see the Old One now and then,
> And try to keep relations on the level.
> It's really decent of so great a person
> To talk so humanely, even to the Devil."

> "Here stand I, ach, Philosophy
> Behind me, and Law and Medicine, too,
> And, to my cost, Theology—
> All these I have sweated through and through,
> And now you see me a poor fool
> As wise as when I started school!"

Except during occasional interruptions from Mac-Neice ("Mephisto, point up 'decent.' . . . Faust, point down 'ach' "), the poetry continued to vibrate and resound in the studio, but when Faust's assistant made his entrance into the study, the drama came to a stop. "The door should be medieval—heavy and stiff on its hinges," the producer said to the engineer, "but it sounds modern." None of the recordings from the sound-effects library of the B.B.C. were right; it required the mixing of two records—the scraping of a bunch of keys on a table and the shuffling of a chair—to reproduce, many minutes later, the lumbering door. It was, however, the arrangement of the effects for Easter Sunday that caused the longest delay. Recordings of bells—from Indian cowbells to the bells of the Cologne Cathedral—were assembled and reassembled, until there was an epiphany of sound, a flood of joyous clanging. Half an hour later, with one sound succeeding another, Easter was born to the slow, uneven strokes of Angelus bells.

At seven o'clock in the evening, following four days of rehearsal, the master tape was to be cut. Up until the last minute, words were being pointed up and down, and sound effects were being synchronized. When the time arrived, from somewhere in the depths of Broadcasting House the engineers signalled that they were ready. The players coughed and cleared their throats, and Mac-Neice's daughter arrived just in time to take her place in a private listening booth. The play was on its way. Everyone on MacNeice's side of the partition sat following his script and marking muffed passages. Now Faust, instead of saying "Or float with spirits round mountain grottoes," said "*down* mountain grottoes." Now the sound effects didn't match the lines. Now an actor signalled that he wasn't happy with a speech. At the end of the recording, such passages were retaken, to be edited into the master tape later.

For the past two years, the Third has broadcast, under the general title "Dunford Dialogues," a series of informal intellectual discussions. These conversations are supposed to differ from the usual finish and polish of Third lectures as pine does from ebony, to give listeners a sense of coming into contact with some distinguished contemporary minds in a manner that suggests brushing against the knots and bark of raw wood. Renford Bambrough, tutor and assistant lecturer in classics at St. John's College, Cambridge, recently recalled how the Dialogues came about: "David Edge, on one of his talent-scout visits to our Senior Common Room, asked me what I thought of the Third's philosophical offerings. I said that they seemed to be so careful and scripted that they left an impression of artificiality; they turned into unapologetic dissertations on one point of view. For myself, I preferred something more spontaneous. After some discussion, Edge and I arrived at a scheme for gathering—for a few days each year—a number of thinkers in a country house and catching their words and thoughts on a tape recorder. For a first general topic, we settled upon 'The Brain,' and decided to ask some philosophers and scientists to come out to Richard Cobden's estate, in Dunford, to talk about it. Our first assembly, in the spring of 1961, yielded a rich harvest—twelve hours of tape, which typed out to three hundred and sixty pages. In subsequent months, Edge edited the script and recordings down to four forty-five-minute 'Dunford Dialogues.' They came over the Third like a charm."

One sunny day, seven theologians and philosophers

convened in Cobden's house, near Midhurst, in Sussex, for a second series of "Dunford Dialogues." The house—Cobden's furniture and library and a valuable collection of his papers are intact there—is typically English and country. It stands in an estate of a hundred and seventy acres, which is almost half woodland, and it is complete with vinery, solarium, and coach house as well as with such modern conveniences as central heating and mechanized kitchens. (The B.B.C. is one of many social and political groups that use the estate as a retreat.) In the library and the drawing room, where the philosophers and theologians reclined in easy chairs and talked, and in a side room, where the B.B.C. engineers were stationed, the mood was one of gentility and dispassionate thinking. Donald MacKay (professor of communications, University of Keele), Donald MacKinnon (professor of divinity, Cambridge), Ninian Smart (professor of theology, Birmingham University), Father Laurence Bright (a Dominican friar of Blackfriars, Cambridge), John Wisdom (professor of philosophy, Cambridge), the Reverend David Cox (vicar of All Saints, Chatham, Kent), and Renford Bambrough talked for four days, often continuously from morning to evening—sometimes in groups of three or four, sometimes all seven together—and the names of philosophers and religious figures were often on their lips. When they were not tackling designated themes with such working titles as "The Greek Gods," "Ancient and Modern Philosophy," "Existentialism: Is There Any Such Thing?," "Theological Language and Scientific Language," "Persons and Things," "Personal Knowledge," "Something and Nothing," and "The Way, the Truth, and the Life," they slept, played croquet, and went on long walks. When this series of the "Dialogues" was in its last day, and only one evening summation discussion—"God and Science," to be led by Wisdom—remained on the agenda, all the participants except Wisdom gathered in the dining room for B.B.C. sherry and dinner. In one corner, the producer, Edge—tall and thin, his speech as disarming as a Boy Scout badge he was wearing in his buttonhole—was conversing with MacKinnon, a Scot, whose deep, booming voice filled the large room. As the Cambridge professor talked, he continuously sharpened pencils with a razor blade; he carried a supply of blades in his pocket, and the pencils, thanks to the B.B.C., awaited him wherever he turned. He often inadvertently dropped a used blade on the floor, and Edge picked up after him as inconspicuously as possible. At one point, the producer and the professor talked about the absent Wisdom. Ever since Wisdom had agreed, the previous night, to lead the final discussion, he had kept to his room, descending only for his part in other dialogues and for a quick lunch and tea— both of which he took in silence. He had supplanted Cobden as the house ghost, and his name was passed around among the company of thinkers as though he were a legendary captain and they his doting sailors.

"Wisdom was a star pupil of Wittgenstein," MacKinnon said. (Since Ludwig Wittgenstein, a philosopher of European origins and Cambridge Common Room renown, published his "Tractatus Logico-Philosophicus" in 1922, he has perhaps had more influence than anyone else upon the lives and the thinking of philosophers in the English-speaking world.) "Like Wittgenstein—or, for that matter, Socrates—even at this moment John is probably carrying on an audible struggle with his thoughts," MacKinnon continued. "John, like his master, thinks aloud, and has never quite outgrown his shyness of setting pen to paper. Perhaps because he doesn't write much, his utterances carry the weight of his big, restless mind."

"But, unlike Wittgenstein, Professor Wisdom is a great horse enthusiast," Edge said. "His first remark after seeing the estate was 'I'm sorry I left my horse behind.'"

"Indeed, he often visits Newmarket," MacKinnon said.

"You'll see, he'll bring up betting in every conversation," Bambrough said, coming up. "A little while ago, he was at the University of Virginia, and he impressed the students as much by his horsemanship as by his philosophy."

At the tinkle of a bell, the dialogists took their places at the dinner table. Soon a gentleman with a thin face and with tufts of bushy hair wrapping up his ears materialized. He was Wisdom. During dinner, he broke his silence only once. Turning to MacKinnon, whose voice still had possession of the room, he said, "I see the art of preaching has not died in Scotland." Everyone, including MacKinnon, laughed.

Wisdom didn't stay for coffee but returned to his room. Half an hour later, when it was time for the recording to start, he reappeared. Coffee cups were hastily put away, tape recorders were turned on, and, once the thinkers had settled in sofas and chairs, lit their pipes or cigars, and served themselves port, they began talking. The setting, while perhaps not as festive as that of Plato's dialogues, was nevertheless a sufficient lubricant for the questioning minds; it gave a sense of world enough and time. At first, Wisdom did not speak, but when he did, his voice, not much louder than a whisper, mesmerized all. Though his halting sentences came across like so many raps on a door of knowledge, his words—individual and distinct—suggested those of a medium more than those of a professor: "At the heart of what Jesus said was what he said about God the Father, the Father in Heaven, about how He cared, and does and will help us—His power to save us. This is not unlike what some other religious teachers have said. If anyone should feel impatient with one who complains that he cannot understand what Jesus said, then this person feeling impatient should, I think, begin by re-marking this very simple point: that what Jesus said is in some way metaphorical. A child told that he has another father might well begin to look, listen for, or wait for such a person, and if he did begin to do this, then, as we talk about God, we should have to explain to him that he shouldn't expect to see a person or be able to talk to a person as he can to his own father. In trying to make clear some remarks as to what Jesus meant . . . about God and about His relation to us, we compared them with statements made about gods by the Greeks, because these were a little less strange, less metaphorical, in that at any rate some of the Greeks, some of the time, didn't regard it as out of the question that they should see the gods of whom they spoke."

He went on to talk about the proofs of scientific and religious statements: "Amongst the cases that come before a court are some where the trouble does not arise through any lack in the information before us—we have what we need before us—and yet there is still a question, and this question is, again, not like that sort of question which comes before an accountant, who is provided with all the information he needs, and the accountant, though he doesn't need to look further, has a very definite technique for arriving at a very definite conclusion. . . . [This is] the procedure that must be used by lawyers in difficult questions as to whether a man knew the risk that he ran in doing the work he did. These questions lack . . . that feature which explains the difficulty of conflict between people when the data they have available is incomplete, and one thinks that when new and further data comes in, this will settle the matter in his favor, and the other thinks that further data will settle it in his. . . . I'm not suggesting that the question about God is one to which further experience is irrelevant, though we may tend to wonder what now can be done to decide whether the theory of continuous creation is the right one or not, and whether, even when the new data comes along, it won't still be possible to maintain both these theories in the face of it, and still be hoping for more data to come in. Still, there it is. There are still experiments to be done which will be relevant to the matter, however much it may be true that Einstein said, when the astronomers disputed observations on the perihelion of Mercury, 'Whatever the absurdities, it's a damn good theory'—which reminds us very, very forcibly of his point that conflict between one scientist and another is by no means always like the conflict between a man who thinks a certain horse is going to win and one who thinks he isn't. Scientists have sometimes been too much represented, if not by themselves . . . by logicians and philosophers, as a sort of super bookmakers. . . ."

Wisdom and the other dialogists talked on into the night. The producer took notes, marking the knotted passages in order to shape the broadcast on the B.B.C.'s anvil.

On a day soon after the recording of "Faust," MacNeice left Broadcasting House to lunch at a nearby pub—Shirreffs Wine Parlour, off Oxford Circus. Martin Esslin was already there, and so were some of the "Faust" cast, talking about new parts with other producers. Indeed, it appeared that the clientele of the pub was almost entirely writers, producers, and actors who at one time or another worked for the Corporation. The customers drank, jostled, and talked, mostly about the B.B.C.

FIRST PRODUCER: I am against putting culture in different streams. I would rather have a cultural mixed drink on all three services.

SECOND PRODUCER: If only the Third was interested in bringing the light to the ordinary man!

THIRD PRODUCER: Yes. We get first-rate talkers, but the question is, How many listen to them? We function sometimes in a vacuum, remain in the backwaters of broadcasting journalism.

FOURTH PRODUCER: I agree. Orwell used to say that

the creative life of any great venture is ten or fifteen years. If we are to prove him wrong, we must ceaselessly make an effort to connect with new generations of listeners.

FIFTH PRODUCER: I have a slightly different attack. I would rather have the program run by one person—like a good journal—and do away with compromises and bickering between the buyers and sellers.

FIRST WRITER: I like radio because there is no Lord Chamberlain to please.

SECOND WRITER: But there are the governors to please. Someone told me that the Corporation refused to produce Beckett's "Endgame" in English because, in its Lord's Prayer, God was called a *"salaud"*—which in Beckett's own English version was translated "bastard." Beckett wouldn't hear of changing "bastard" to "dirty man."

THIRD WRITER: Is that why they broadcast it in French?

SECOND WRITER: Yes. After the stage success in England, Beckett let the Corporation have its way with "dirty man."

FIRST ACTOR: Certain of us, without the B.B.C., would be jobless.

SECOND ACTOR: Such as the dumpy, frowzy middle-aged ladies who would dissolve playhouses into titters but whose Juliets and Oliver Twists can bring tears to the eyes of radio audiences.

MacNeice, who had been holding forth to friends in a corner, now talked a little, between sips of hock, about being a Third producer. He said that on the Third a producer could stage more masterpieces in a year than he would be able to put on in the commercial theatre in a lifetime. The B.B.C. left one alone. It provided the stability of a salary and the independence of an organization made up for the most part of artists. "But many of us work not for the salary—it compares more to a don's than to an entertainer's—but for love," he went on. "There is a kind of excitement in having a few hundred pounds in your pocket, so to speak, to produce a program in any way you wish. In earlier times, we producers used to listen quite a lot to each other's programs. The old hands would drop in on the studios of the younger producers to criticize their broadcasts. Indeed, we were trained by the light of their advice, and, of course, by the listeners—our box office—who are polled by the audience-research people. Since the cuts in time and the loss of audiences to television, a general depression has set in, and radio, while still the yeast of culture here, is not what it used to be."

In another corner, Esslin was talking to a nervous, taut youth who had had his first acting job with the Corporation in "Faust." Although the broadcast was still two weeks away, the actor was worrying about the reviews and the listener response. Esslin was calming him by meticulously explaining the mechanics developed by the B.B.C. for polling and measuring the listening population of a particular program. A sampling of listeners from different classes and intellectual backgrounds was interviewed; their comments were weighed and graded so that in the effort to arrive at a numerical appreciation index for a broadcast the remarks of a university lecturer counted more than those of a farmer. "Here is a typical report on our recent broadcast of the new translation of the Oresteian Trilogy," Esslin said, pulling some papers out of his pocket. He went on to read some of the listeners' comments: "A research scientist says of the plays, 'The translation was mostly adequate, but occasionally lapsed into bathos and banality.' According to a commercial artist, however, 'the sheer grandeur of Aeschylus' *did* come through very well. A farmer agrees, and says that the broadcast was 'an experience I would not have missed.' And a university lecturer? 'As a non-classical scholar, this was the best presentation of Greek tragedy I have heard on radio,' he says."

Inside the Parlour, the editor of the *Times* seemed to be present in spirit.

1963

1971. A choleric friend who covers the B.B.C. for a London paper writes, "Alas, your description of the Third Programme has become a historical record of a cultural phenomenon that could not survive the dawn of the nineteen-seventies. Even the name 'Third Programme' disappeared early last year in a burst of controversy both inside and outside the corridors of the B.B.C. This storm is indicative of the crisis in British culture and in British politics; the intellectual élite, who were supported by the rule of an aristocracy, are being relentlessly destroyed by Philistines who are supported by petit-bourgeois bureaucrats, just as the great statesmen with vision are being supplanted by mean, small-minded boors."

III

Quiet, Beneficent Things

THE BOOK TRADE EVERYWHERE GIVES THE IMpression of being weak in the knees. Big publishers are ingesting little ones, firms that have no interest in or knowledge of books are taking over old-established houses, and those publishers who, as a matter of course, continue to bring out good books are being forced to rely increasingly for their profits on best-sellers, reference books, and such subsidiary rights as book clubs, serializations, and films. Similarly, booksellers, who, in a sense, are the better half of the trade (in the United States they receive from twenty-five to fifty per cent of the published price of a book, while the publisher's share is from twenty to forty per cent and the author's is from ten to fifteen per cent), seem to be in the throes of some malaise in regard to both the number and the types of books stocked. When men of the book trade are approached for the reasons, they say that even though today there are more readers, and more books, both paperback and hardcover, to buy and read, practically no business has found the present, with its emphasis on self-service and mass selling, less hospitable than serious bookselling; unlike a greengrocer, the bookseller cannot leave his customers to serve themselves, for searching out a title is like looking for a particular tiger in a vast jungle. In the business, serious bookselling is sometimes defined as "placing a worthy book in a worthy hand"—a rather Victorian sentiment. But then the serious bookseller has been a dying breed almost since the turn of the century. The truth of this assertion becomes apparent if one studies the operations of such a bookseller, because, being a sort of weathervane for the changing winds of people's reading habits and publishers' preoccupations, he is blown hither and thither in a way that makes him a sound indicator of the major problems besetting the book business.

B. H. Blackwell, Ltd., of Oxford, may be the best bookshop in the world, and it is certainly one of the few serious bookshops left. On a recent representative day, Blackwell's received mail orders from forty-three countries, counting Britain, for 3,198 items, ranging from "The Tale of Mrs. Tittlemouse" to Tertullian's "Treatise Against Praxeas," and from the "Transactions of the Convention on Thermonuclear Processes, Proceeding Part A, Supplement No. 2" (published by the Institution of Electrical Engineers) to the "Workshop Manual of the Humber Hawk Saloon Mk. VI." Of these, 2,786 orders were for general books printed in Great Britain, and the rest, 412, for music, foreign publications, and second-hand items. Almost exactly half of the requests could be filled from stock. For the others—a total of 1,598 books—the shop had to communicate with two hundred and forty-six publishers, who, in reply, supplied 1,085 and reported that 513 were "binding," "reprinting," "out of stock," "out of print," or "not yet published." Blackwell's now had the duty of recording these titles in what is intramurally called a "file of dues," in the hope that it might obtain the books later, and of informing its customers of their present unavailability.

Any one order can plummet a Blackwell's assistant into exasperating and befuddling research, for every year in Britain alone some two hundred major publishers (if the minor ones are included, the number rises to fifteen hundred) release twenty-three thousand [now about twenty-five thousand] new titles and new editions, and let many thousands go out of print. The difficulty of simply classifying new books is suggested by the fact that seven decimal places have been added to the original three of the Dewey decimal system since it was evolved, in 1876. A Blackwell's assistant might begin his search by looking for the book on the premises (there are a hundred thousand [now two hundred and fifty thousand] volumes, new and old, on the shelves), go on to Whitaker's Reference Catalogue of Current Literature (it comes out every four or five years, twelve months behind) and then to Whitaker's Annual Cumulative Booklist (it trails by only four months), and turn next to the British National Bibliography, in the hope that, since it reports all books deposited in the British Museum for copyright purposes, it might include out-of-the-way books not recorded in either of the Whitakers. If the book should still escape him, he might have to press on to Wilson's Cumulative Book Index (an American publication attempting to record all books published anywhere in the world), to the partial index of books appearing in the *Bookseller*, to Blackwell's own indexes, made from various sources and covering forthcoming titles and obscure publications, and, finally, to the back numbers of Wilson and Whitaker. After this chase, it might turn out that the customer made a significant misspelling, gave the title of the review instead of the title of the book, gave the Christian name of the author instead of his surname, or—the last indignity—gave the name of the reviewer instead of the name of the author. Publishers, for their part, announce books that they do not publish, announce them under one title and publish them under another, or don't announce them at all. Yet the greatest hazards facing a bookseller come not from the publisher, or even from the public, but from the books themselves: titles may be misleading (Trotman-Dickenson's "Free Radicals" is to be looked for not in the political section but among the books on physical chemistry, and Duffin's "Amphibians" and Davie's "Articulate Energy" not in science but in English literature); titles may change in midstream (Robson's "Problems of Nationalized Industries" appears in a revised edition as "Nationalized Industry and Public Ownership"); volumes of the same work may have different publishers (the first volume of de Gaulle's war memoirs was published in Britain by Collins and the second and third volumes by Weidenfeld & Nicolson); titles may have parts not corresponding to the volume numbers (Books II and III of Wyndham Lewis's "The Human Age" are contained in one volume); two works may have similar titles (Oman's "History of the Art of War in the Middle Ages," priced at ten pounds, is not to be confused with Oman's "Art of War in the Middle

70]

Ages," priced at fourteen shillings); the same work may have different titles (the paperback edition of Kingsley Amis's "That Uncertain Feeling" is called "Only Two Can Play," the name of the film based on the book); and various editions may have the same title (does the customer for Blegen's "Troy" require the three available volumes of the four-volume set, at forty-three pounds four shillings, or the facsimile from the new edition of the "Cambridge Ancient History," at three shillings sixpence, or—to put the problem more generally—does any customer want the full, the intermediate, the abridged, the clothbound, the paperbound, the illustrated, the unillustrated, the annotated, the unannotated, the original, or the translated edition of any given work?). The gravamen of the serious bookseller's case is that whereas even omnibus shops, like the chain of Marks & Spencer, handle five thousand items at the outside—and perhaps no more than a thousand, excluding the small variations in sizes and colors—a serious bookseller has to be prepared to supply any one of the two hundred and fifty thousand titles, by seventy-five thousand authors, that are in print at any one time. And this holds true even though the total annual turnover of the British book trade is only about a hundred million pounds [now about a hundred and fifty million]—in America it is seven hundred and fifty million dollars—whereas that of Marks & Spencer is three times as high.

Ever since the beginning of the twentieth century, with its businesses dealing in enormous quantities of merchandise, and its customers buying with shopping carts, the services asked of a good bookseller have borne less and less relation to the price paid for them. In America, clumps of serious booksellers remain in a few metropolises and, rather strangely, in the recesses of department stores, which have conjured up something called "loss-leader departments," whereby less profitable items are carried but are strategically placed in the remotest corners of the floor, in the hope that customers for them will be waylaid at some point by more profitable merchandise, and losses sustained in one department will be recouped in another. In Britain, while the good bookshops in small towns are also a thing of the past, a handful of booksellers—mainly in cities—have assumed a new role and a new prosperity by turning themselves through the years into vast mail-order houses and supplying books to, for instance, countries in the Empire that were founding new universities and new libraries. But many booksellers feel that the primary reason good bookshops, however few, still exist in Britain, whereas they seem to have died out almost completely in America, has to do with discounts. In America, the prevalence of discounts on books with good sales possibilities has the effect of discouraging the bookseller from stocking books that do not have a quick turnover, but Britain has a so-called Net Book Agreement—a gentleman's agreement among publishers and booksellers to stand firm on discounts and to stabilize the margin of profits on books— and this, by removing price competition, has made possible the kind of service demanded by the peculiar nature of books as merchandise. (If a book is exported, the total bookseller profit is forty-five per cent, of which the British bookseller gets a third, the remainder going to

the foreign bookseller handling the book in his country;
if it is sold in Britain, the profit is usually twenty-five per
cent, or even less, on a book "of an educational nature,"
and also on a book with general appeal, unless the book
is ordered before the publication date, when the profit is
thirty-three and a third per cent, the difference of eight
and a third per cent being due to the fact that in the first
case the publisher is deemed to be sharing some of the
retailing function of the bookseller, whereas in the second case the shop is taking an additional risk, for in
Britain, as opposed to the United States, the bookseller
cannot return his unsold stock.) The first book with a
fixed price was Alfred Marshall's "Principles of Eco-
nomics," published by Macmillan in 1890, and not until
about a quarter of a century afterward were all the
publishers brought into line. The Agreement was made
possible only by the circumstance that the agents of the
Crown chose to overlook its plainly monopolistic aspects. In June, 1962, the Agreement was reviewed in the
Restrictive Practices Court, and, not surprisingly, the
best defense for the fixing of prices came from Richard
Blackwell, who is the son and heir of Sir Basil Blackwell,
the current head of the shop in Oxford.

It is our experience [he said] that if a bookseller takes reasonable care to see that he is not landed with an undue proportion
of out-of-the-way items from any customer, he can, after giving
good service over the swings and roundabouts alike . . . find
himself at the end of a year with a profit, which, though modest,
will recompense him for his labours.
For this he must, in particular, be grateful, because any system of charging for the multifarious services that he renders
would present a most formidable and intractable problem. It

would be difficult to determine where his services begin and end. Should he, for example, charge customers for the extensive use they make of his stock, sometimes reading the very book which he requires to fill an order he has received by post, and which therefore must be ordered from the publisher? Should he charge for the research required by some customer's query about the availability of a book which he does not, in the event, order? Should he charge for the specialized knowledge which enables him to answer a question which might defeat another bookseller? Could he, as a result of ordering a book (after considerable research), having it reported reprinting, informing the customer, recording the order, reviewing it periodically, and eventually being told by the publisher that it was definitely out of print, send the customer a bill for doing his utmost to obtain a book but, through no fault of his own, failing?

The monopolists won the case, and thus received legal sanction for an essentially illegal practice. (Recently, the Conservative and Labour parties, courting the consumers and giving way to the pressures of supermarkets and "multiple stores," both came out against "resale price maintenance." [The booksellers successfully defended themselves in court, and resale price maintenance is still in effect today.]) As one of them left the courtroom, he quoted a pronouncement of Richard Blackwell's: "The value of a healthy book trade must . . . be measured not only by the criteria of cost and convenience, but also of culture: for the book trade is not concerned merely with manufactured articles, but with the things which, in Antigone's words, 'live not for today and yesterday, but for ever.' "

Today, the book trade is healthier—as these things go—in Britain than in any other English-speaking country, the probable, and paradoxical, reason being that eighty per cent of the entire national business is carried on by about twenty per cent of the booksellers, the serious ones (in the opinion of most) being W. & G. Foyle, Ltd., J. & E. Bumpus, Ltd., and Dillon's University Bookshop, Ltd., in London; W. Heffer & Sons, Ltd., in Cambridge; George's Sons, Ltd., in Bristol; James Thin, Ltd., in Edinburgh; and Blackwell's, in Oxford—and, in a sense, also W. H. Smith & Son, Ltd., which now owns the old Cambridge bookshop of Bowes & Bowes and has bookshops and bookstalls throughout Britain. These booksellers, on account of their dominance, can afford to give the same ungrudging attention to slow movers that they do to fast ones. Yet not all the members of even this small group choose to do so, one or another preferring to make extra money on the side on the "swings" of book clubs and publishing. They all do have a distinctive character, perhaps because they are family firms and indulge in inbreeding, conducting themselves as though they alone were pedigreed and all the other bookshops were mongrels.

Foyle's, which, according to its advertisements, has "the largest bookselling business of its kind in the world," got started early in this century, when two teenage boys, William (Willie) Alfred Foyle and his younger brother, Gilbert, bought a couple of dozen textbooks in order to study for a civil-service examination. They failed the examination, but, with the help of an advertisement in an educational periodical, succeeded in selling their books from their home, in the London suburb of Shoreditch. Having tasted the pleasures of the trade, they renewed their stock and went into business. As it expanded, they outgrew first the family kitchen, where they kept their books, and then successive shops in Islington and Peckham, and finally settled down in a shop on Charing Cross Road, in the heart of London. Today, the Charing Cross business, housed in a clutter of five shabby buildings, almost outdoes Texas in the fervor of its self-congratulation. Daily advertisements—probably the only ones of *their* kind in the world—point over and over to certain advantages: four acres of floor space, thirty miles of shelves, four million volumes, seven hundred employees, an annual turnover of some three million pounds, and ten book clubs (with a combined membership of three hundred thousand, each of whom is committed to buying one book a month for six months). Foyle's also announces, with an equal air of pride, that each week it dispatches four tons of books, mostly legal and medical, to paper mills for pulping. These various boasts have become so much a part of Foyle's legend that when, in 1964, the *Times* came to write an obituary of Willie Foyle—and obituaries are one of the paper's strongest departments—it did little but quote them.

Mrs. Ronald Batty, née Christina Agnes Lillian Foyle, who is the daughter and heiress of Willie Foyle, not long ago talked about Foyle's to a visitor to her apartment, which is on the second floor of Foyle's main building. Her manner was disarming. "Most of the assistants on our sales staff are girls who come to us for a year before going up to the university or getting married, or they are from the Continent, having come to this country to learn English," she said. "The assistants who do stay a little longer with us and manage to learn something about their subject tend to build a department round their interest and then leave. In the Oriental department, an assistant may build up a good selection of books in Hindi one year, and the next year an assistant who knows a lot about Japanese may take charge, with the result that the Hindi books simply lie on the shelves— probably this second assistant can't even read the titles. Then, we have clerks who are not very good at dealing with requests for titles by post. When my father was alive, he used to look over many of the letters, and would often remember a title that the clerk had said was not in existence. My father had a very good memory, but he took it with him, and I can't supervise the correspondence. My time is taken up in running Foyle's monthly literary lunches and our many book clubs. If you ask why we don't have good assistants—well, salaries of the kind we can pay our assistants do not attract persons looking for careers. Now, Blackwell's, in Oxford, and Heffer's, in Cambridge, have an easier time, because a lot of people like living in those cities and will therefore consent to work for lower salaries. We are in the heart of the metropolis and can't offer amenities. We even have to employ detectives. Being in the middle of Soho, which is notorious around the world for its sales of pornography, we sometimes get a strange clientele. There are always people here sniffing books. And there are gangsters who threaten to destroy books unless they are paid off."

Foyle's complete aloofness from the public it serves has given rise to some lampoons. One of the latest appeared last year in the satirical weekly called *Private Eye* and summed up the advantages of shopping at Foyle's like this:

> One of the Londoner's favourite pastimes is the old sport of "Book Browsing." . . .
> Foils . . . is indeed the Mecca of the bookloving Londoner. Here he can "browse" at peace, forgetting for a moment the cares and anxieties of the outside world.
> Foils makes it well nigh impossible for the visitor to alight at once on the book of his choice, as this may spoil his enjoyment. . . .
> Although the books are placed under headings, these are not at first sight in any way appropriate. To understand them the "browser" must learn a "satirical" code which is used—thus "Anthropology" = "Music," and "History" = "Gardening." Colourful "assistants" specially selected for their inability to speak English stand at vantage points to see that the "browsers" are not disturbed.
> Should a visitor decide to actually "buy" a book—a practice which is actively discouraged—he must travel the whole length of the building in order to pay for it. During his absence he may find that the "assistant" and the book have colourfully "vanished."

It is hardly surprising that the best bookshops should be not in the metropolis of London but in Oxford and Cambridge, or that their booksellers should reflect in some measure the tribal differences between the two universities. The stock of the main Cambridge bookseller, Heffer's, is, like the university it serves, alive to all branches of science; what dead spots it has lie in areas of the humanities. Also, Heffer's, like the city of Cambridge, makes a clear distinction between town and gown, running separate establishments for the goats and the sheep. At 18 Sidney Street is Heffer's stationers, carrying typewriters, envelopes for wages, cellophane tape, and popular books. Nearby, at 3-4 Petty Cury, there is another Heffer's, the soul of the firm, which stocks only books. If the first supplies low-priced editions of the Bible and picture books on birds, the second handles works on theology and ornithology. The scholarly atmosphere of the Petty Cury establishment is due at least partly to R. G. Heffer, a rather easygoing product of Corpus Christi College, Cambridge, who became the overseer of the firm when his father died, in 1948. R. G. Heffer takes pride in being deficient in drive and ambition, and preens himself on certain archaic features of his bookshop. From the day a customer opens an account, a file containing all his mail-order requests for books is kept by a salesclerk of the department dealing in his special field just on the chance that the customer may stop in at the shop, in which case the clerk, having consulted the correspondence files, can chat with the client about his reading interests. (At Foyle's, according to legend, the correspondence is burned each month, so that if anyone writes in saying "Six months ago, I sent you a pound. What has happened to my order?" he is automatically sent a pound or a book, with no questions asked.) In Heffer's view, the swings that have enabled his Petty Cury bookshop to provide the old-fashioned type of service, handling fast- and slow-selling titles on an equal footing, have been the profits on his Sidney Street shop, a sizable remainder business he does on the side, and, most important, the low rent he has been paying for shelf space; his landlord until recently was Emmanuel College, which was more interested in patronage and worthy tenants than in money. Now, however, Heffer's is a tenant of a group of London property developers, who are interested in making the most profitable use of their land, and Heffer has resigned himself to the fact that his Petty Cury shop may someday have to move into a new, compact building and pay three or four times as much for shelf space as it pays now. Heffer is sure that his firm is strong and prosperous enough to survive the higher rents, but, all the same, in this respect he is uneasy. [The Petty Cury shop was in fact recently moved to new premises, on Trinity Street.]

As for Blackwell's, on Oxford's Broad Street, to Bishop William Stubbs, one of the half-dozen most influential scholars in nineteenth-century Oxford, it was "the literary man's public house," and to the critic Marghanita Laski, when she was an undergraduate at Oxford fifty years later, it was "the best bookshop in the world, where no one ever disturbed you and you could, if you wished, simply sit in a corner and read books right through." John Masefield, Poet Laureate of Britain, must have had people like Miss Laski in mind when he wrote:

> There, in the Broad, within whose booky house
> Half England's scholars nibble books or browse.
> Where'er they wander, blessed fortune theirs:
> Books to the ceiling, other books upstairs;
> Books, doubtless, in the cellar, and behind
> Romantic bays, where iron ladders wind.

Indeed, as the *Observer* once put it, speaking for Oxonians, "When the exile returns to Oxford, after years abroad, he visits his College—and Blackwell's. It is more than a great bookshop; it is an institution."

The first mention of B. H. Blackwell is in the Oxford Directory of 1846, which lists a bookseller of that name as operating a shop at 46 High Street, St. Clements—just across the Magdalen Bridge and so just outside the city's eastern limit. In those days, one had to be a freeman or the son or apprentice of a freeman, or else pay a fine—an obsolete guild impost dating from the Middle Ages—in order to set up a business within the limits of Oxford. The aspiring merchant Benjamin Harris Blackwell apparently refused on principle to meet the terms of this impost, and so was forced to found his business far out from the center of Oxford, thereby restricting the scope of his shop so severely that when he died, after ten years of diligence, it perished with him; the probators put the value of the stock at only a hundred and fifty-three pounds and five shillings. Since there were at least twenty-one other booksellers serving Oxford at the time—two of them, Thornton's and Parker's, so well established that they were almost beyond the threat of competition—Benjamin may never have had a chance. The meagre accounts of his life show him to have taken more than an ordinary interest in books (he was one of the co-founders of the Oxford Public Library, of which he became the first librarian) and to have been a man of principle (a total abstainer, he defied the government by refusing to pay the liquor tax of the day). If family legend can be trusted, he had a notably sweet disposition. In his later years, he suffered from some kind of ailment that afflicted him with stabs of pain, and it is said that so as not to alarm his wife when he cried out, he would always sing down the scale immediately afterward. Mrs. Blackwell, who survived her husband by thirty years, was determined that the family should reënter the bookselling trade, but she was compelled to approach her ambition indirectly. She had some talent for needlework, and the fashion of the day called for undergraduates to wear embroidered waistcoats, so she began taking the garments in, and brought up her children—two boys and a girl—on the proceeds. As soon as her eldest child, who was named after his father and was called Harry, reached the age of thirteen (the year was 1862), she took him out of school and bound him as an apprentice to a bookseller for seven years, starting at a shilling a week, and thereby laid the foundations of the second—and the present—house of Blackwell's. Harry used the dead hours of his apprenticeship to good advantage, memorizing the catalogues of Bernard Quaritch—one of the greatest of the Victorian booksellers and cataloguers—so thoroughly that to the end of his life, if he found a book in his hand that he had not seen before, he would more than likely recognize it from the description he had read in an early Quaritch. Then, at twenty, he became an assistant to another bookseller, with an address on High Street. Ten years later, in 1879, he started his own business, renting and moving into premises consisting of a shop and a back room, with the use of a cellar, at 50 Broad Street, and soon he extended his operations to the ground floor of the adjacent 51 Broad Street, and converted its upstairs into living quarters. The two houses, which had back courtyards and cottages for storage, and were bounded on the west by Trinity College and on the east by a tailor shop and a picture shop, are described in "An Inventory of the Historical Monuments in the City of Oxford" as dating from the time of Queen Anne and comprising "three stories with cellars and attics." The description continues, "The walls are timber-framed and the roofs slate-covered. It [the structure] was built or largely rebuilt as two houses early in the eighteenth century. . . . The front has rusticated angles, a cornice, and two pedimented dormer-windows in the hipped roof. Inside the building are two original stair-cases with turned balusters, close strings, and square newels." Harry opened his shop with a capital of a hundred and fifty pounds, lent to him by a friend at three per cent interest, and with a stock valued at a hundred and twenty-six pounds and composed for the most part of second-hand books or sound workaday editions (Aldine, Pickering, Bohn) of representative classics. The two ground floors of the bookshop, which were each twelve feet square and were connected by a dark corridor, were too small for the bookshelves, and the bookshelves were too big for the small stock of books; to fill up the empty spaces on the shelves, Harry laid some of the volumes on their sides. In its first months, Blackwell's was such a congested place that sometimes the bookseller had to go outside to make room for the customers. Then the bookseller asked the chairman of Barclays Bank for a loan to buy the premises. The banker had misgivings, and at one point inquired, "Well, Mr. Blackwell, are you beginning to capture your rivals' trade?" The bookseller replied, "I believe that there is enough for all." He got the money. With it he expanded his floor space.

Not long ago, Sir Basil Blackwell wrote, "Those who came in from the cobbled street, resonant with iron-shod wheel and 'bright and battering sandal,' found quiet and an invitation, not so much spoken as conveyed by the friendly spirit of the young bookseller, to scrutinize and handle the books on his shelves with no sense of obligation to buy." Harry Blackwell had a shrewd business head. It was to the interest of any Oxford bookseller to dissuade his customer from either paying cash or meeting his bill until at least the middle of the term following his purchase, for a customer who did pay up promptly received a twenty-five-per-cent discount on his books. Harry Blackwell must have been persuasive in encouraging credit, for Benjamin Jowett himself, when he was Master of Balliol, bought "Universal History," by Diodorus Siculus, in November, 1879, and did not pay for it until March, 1881. (Though the practice of offering discounts was ended by the Net Book Agreement, the tradition of credit is so deeply entrenched at Blackwell's that today a hundred and twenty thousand customers regularly buy there on that basis.) Again, Harry judiciously refused to think of marriage until his shop had proved itself a success. By then, he was in his late thirties, and his mother, who lived until she was sixty-two, was in her late fifties. With her encouragement, he took as his wife Miss Lydia Taylor, the last of five daughters of a Norfolk farmer, who, in her turn, had been waiting "until she had fulfilled her vow to see her parents comfortably out of life," as Sir Basil puts it. God, too, had a place in Harry's life. Once, Harry Blackwell bought some books from a widow and later discovered tucked away among them a valuable pamphlet not paid for. He thereupon sent the woman a check, with a note of apology for overlooking the find in the first place, only to draw from her a veiled charge of cheating. She wrote him a stinging letter to the effect that if he should come across any other such unpaid-for finds, she would be grateful for more checks. Mrs. Blackwell, Sr., in a rage against the ingrate, told her son not to indulge in any more such acts of generosity. Harry said, "It doesn't matter what the widow thinks; I want to be on the right side of God." (Basil, his heir, earned his first money by reciting at sixpence a round the Fifteenth Psalm: "Lord, who shall dwell in thy tabernacle . . .") This care for the good will of God lent Blackwell's an air of probity from the very start. In Lord Rosebery's words, the place was "a remarkable shop, kept by a very remarkable man."

Actually, the success of the Broad Street Blackwell's was probably due as much to the times as to the man. As scholars, as intellectuals in politics, as zealous evangelists going out to convert the heathen, few generations in the history of Britain can hold a candle to the Victorians, many of whom had deep associations with Oxford. The reforms introduced at the end of the eighteenth century had awakened Oxford from at least a century of sleep. A series of Commissions of Inquiry and Parliamentary Acts, beginning in 1854, among other things, set up new schools of examination and ended Oxford's status as the preserve of the Church of England. In the second half of the nineteenth century, the university entered its most learned period. Intellect and achievement became its sole values. Its graduates went out to help build the Empire, to found universities and libraries, and, later on, in the case of Rhodes Scholars, to propagate British values in their own countries. Oxford was the center of an ever-widening circle of British influence, and Blackwell's prospered by its mere proximity to the university. Oxford graduates remembered Blackwell's when they were founding a university in India or Australia, or stocking a library in Canada or the Union of South Africa, and inundated it with orders, so that the upstairs bedrooms, the back courtyards and cottages, and the adjacent shops had to be built and rebuilt to accommodate ever more books and departments. Whenever the two houses began to bulge at the seams, some such subsidiary department as accounts or some such self-contained one as musical literature or children's books was pushed out and housed elsewhere in Oxford. Today, the main part of the trade is still carried on from behind the Queen Anne façade and around the Queen Anne staircases. There is, of course, an obvious difference. If Sir Basil wishes to sit down with his staff to a feast—as he did, in fact, in 1954, on the seventy-fifth anniversary of the firm—he will be joined by two hundred and thirty employees from the Broad Street establishment alone, and a hundred and seventy [now five hundred] from the Blackwell subsidiaries and external departments. In 1924, just before Harry died, *he* would have been joined on a similar occasion by only thirty-six; in 1913, the year Basil Blackwell entered the business, they would have been joined by only twenty-four; and in 1879, and for some time thereafter, Harry would have sat down to a lonely banquet of one.

Sir Basil Blackwell, who is the father of five children—three daughters and two sons—lives and behaves, and even sells books, as though he were under an injunction laid down by the last will and testament of the departed century, and particularly those clauses having to do with the middle class, with the solid values of cricket and the classics, character and the family, country living and gentlemanly conduct, and, above all, an easy confidence in one's ability to tell good from evil, vice from virtue. It all began when Harry Blackwell, determined to give his children—one son and one daughter—the education he had missed, put Basil first in an Oxford boarding and day school kept by a couple of spinsters and then, when he was twelve, in Magdalen College School, a modest foundation lying in the shadow of the west wing of Magdalen College, not very far from his grandfather's St. Clements bookshop. Here, in the society of about a hundred boarders, day boys, and masters, Basil was given a beginner's education in virtue and the classics and was told about such former school lights as Thomas Hobbes (remembered for sprawling and "gapeing on mappes"); William Tyndale, the translator of the New Testament; William Camden, the compiler of "Britannia"; John Foxe, the martyrologist; Cardinal Wolsey; and Sir Thomas More, though in fact history is fuzzy about his schooling. Wherever history was obscure, the boy was encouraged to fill in the gaps with his imagination, and so he liked to think that it was here that Richard Hooker learned to enjoy the Odes of Horace, and John Milton acquired the rudiments of learning. At the bookshop, Basil sat and leafed through Spenser's "Faerie Queene," compared Henry Boyd's and H. F. Cary's translations of Dante's "Inferno," and himself gaped at the strange figure on the title page of Hobbes' "Leviathan," letting his mind be molded more by the books whose pages he idly turned than by those he actually read. (Today, he is apt to hover before his bookshelves without quite knowing which book to take down, and he reads with three books open before him.) As he puts it, he learned to think of books as "quiet, beneficent things making a sheltering world within the world."

When Basil was ready for the university, he looked to Merton. At the time, this college was "a sink of iniquity," and its dean was scouting among the applicants for head boys of good Christian schools—upright, religious characters, never in their cups—to help him reform the place. From examination papers they wrote and interviews he held with them, the dean judged Basil and one Austin Longland, of Radley College, near Abingdon, to be just the two boys he was after, and, by naming each of them a "postmaster" (believed to be a corruption of *"portionista,"* this was Merton's designation for the poor scholars who shared in a meagre style the quarters and the commons of the Fellows), recruited them into his collegiate Salvation Army. At Merton, when Austin and Basil—who became the best of friends for life—were not serving as models for the renegades, they built their characters by rowing for their college, playing rugger, and living frugally. (For lunch, which they ate in their rooms, they often had only Stilton cheese, having bought a whole cheese at the beginning of the term to be eaten to the term's fruity end.) Each winter, the college rewarded them with one dinner of goose, provided ungrudgingly, since the bird made up part of the rent paid on college-owned farms. The education of the two boys was taken in hand by a portly and placid classicist called Walter How, who fancied himself a gifted orator and spoke almost entirely in alliterative sentences, on the order of "Thus Pericles found it impossible to pursue a policy of peaceful penetration," or rhetorical ones, on the order of "The day for which he had been sharpening his sword found him dallying with it in the sheath."

Basil took second-class honors in Greats in 1911, and was then farmed out by his father to the Oxford University Press for a period of sixteen months. In 1913, having finished the apprenticeship that Harry had devised for him, he went to work in the family bookshop. As his first order of business, he courted and wed Marion Christine Soans, a classicist in her own right from London University who was then working as secretary to Gilbert Murray. Next, he tackled the publishing side of the business. Practically from the opening of the Broad Street shop, Blackwell's had been publishing crumbs of Oxford belles-lettres, such as "Mensae Secundae," a pamphlet of verses written by Balliol undergraduates, and *Waifs and Strays*, a magazine of university poetry. To these Basil now added the outpourings of Aldous

Huxley, Dorothy Sayers, and Sacheverell Sitwell, only to see them leave him, upon receiving their degrees, for London agents and London publishers. Once, Robert Bridges visited Basil and admonished him "not to leave the quiet paths of bookselling for the perilous course of publishing," adding, "Anybody can be a publisher, but there is only one Blackwell's." Within a few years of receiving this counsel, though, Basil Blackwell and a partner founded a press in Stratford-upon-Avon and began publishing, among other things, the complete works of the Venerable Bede, Chaucer, and Smollett. In scholarship, the books, which appeared under the imprint of the Shakespeare Head Press, were inferior to workaday editions of the same classics put out by the Oxford University Press, but they were much handsomer, being intended for the libraries of gentlemen's country houses. Nothing gave the young publisher more satisfaction than a letter he received from a country gentleman asking for a replacement of a Shakespeare Head volume of Plutarch because while he was reading that volume over the dinner table he spilled a little wine on it. The stained Plutarch is now cherished as a souvenir—a symbol of the gentry's way with books. The Second World War and the decline of the gentry made Blackwell's turn more and more to publishing children's schoolbooks and scholarly works of such special interest that they could be sold mainly to librarians, through the shop's catalogues.

Blackwell's has remained primarily a bookshop, however, and over the years its character has become more, rather than less, pious and aggressive. Applause for what one might call this Christian-duenna side of the book-shop is probably limited to the families of scholars. In this age of high prices and accelerating obsolescence, even more than before, a scholar's private library has tended to constitute his porcelain, silver, and linen. Not only are scholarly works expensive, even though they are often printed with the aid of subsidies, but they are issued in such small editions that they sometimes go out of print with publication, thereby becoming valuable assets. The scholar's heirs, in the hope of realizing the best price for them, may put up the library for auction. Until less than a decade ago, although the Auctions (Bidding Agreements) Act of 1927 had specifically made collusion in auctions illegal, some antiquarian booksellers were engaged in a conspiracy to keep the bidding down to about ten per cent of the real worth of the books. After an auction was over, they would ad-journ to a pub, where they would hold a private auction of their own, selling the books for their real value to one of their number, and sharing the difference between the rigged price and the true price. Unless collusion could be proved—and proof was almost impossible to obtain—reselling the bought goods was perfectly legal, so the arraigning of members of the so-called book ring seemed for a long time to be out of the question. During this period, Blackwell and other upright booksellers could only instruct their representatives to force the bidding up by offering the top prices, but this procedure natu-rally had its limits. Then came a chance to put teeth in the Auctions Act by means of publicity. In 1956, a trade journal that had been campaigning against the ring for several years was allowed to die when vengeful book-sellers simply neglected to renew their subscriptions. The virtuous booksellers protested this course of action with a vigor that inspired articles in the press and prompted a discussion in Parliament. (One Honourable Member got up and said of the ring, "I hope that the Joint Under-Secretary will voice his strong disapproval of these brigands and tell us how good people can be protected against their maraudings.") Characteristically, Blackwell initiated a crusade of his own, which took the form of a double-barrelled announcement, the first part stating that he had drafted and was circulating for book-sellers' signatures a solemn declaration to the effect that they had never engaged in collusive bidding at auctions and would never do so in the future, and the second part stating that he had persuaded the publishers of the Di-rectory of Dealers in Second-Hand and Antiquarian Books in the British Isles to mark the names of the signatories with asterisks in their next edition. Only sixty-seven dealers out of a total of about eight hundred could be found to sign the declaration—a heavy indictment of the trade, even when allowance was made for those who objected to the method of the declaration on principle. (Their case was strengthened by the fact that Blackwell had infuriatingly dubbed the Directory a "Book of Saints," on the ground that everybody knew of the existence of the ring, just as "the Catholics know the existence of Hell without exactly knowing who is in it.") The International Association of Antiquarian Booksellers was at last moved to put its house in order. It convened a meeting of its members and, in the spirit of "let bygones be bygones," outlawed conspiracies at future auctions and appointed a watchdog committee to enforce the ban. Blackwell was exultant. Not only had his crusade been successful but, in addition, he had been made a knight—or, as he is fond of putting it, had been "sprayed by the fountain of honor." Indeed, as he occasionally points out, he was the first bookseller (or, in his words, "member of a greasy trade") ever to be given a handle to his name, and although in recent years there has been a democratic tendency to honor the top men in their field, regardless of the nature of their work, there can be little doubt that it was Basil Blackwell's virtuous concern for the widows and children of scholars (however strong his wish to see the end of a system that penalized him as a bookseller who held out against the ring) that caught the eye of the government—and, later, of Merton, which elected the knighted bookseller an honorary Fellow.

Unfortunately, the Christian duenna had her tedious side. She was constantly shooing this unseemly book off the premises and giving extra elbowroom to that inspirational pamphlet. And as the profane century has advanced, she has become more rigid rather than less. When Vladimir Nabokov's "Lolita" was published in England, copies were unavailable in Oxford, and *Isis*, which is one of the two main organs of student opinion (the other being *Cherwell*), had something to say about that fact:

"Lolita" was published last Thursday, but there isn't a copy to be found in any Oxford book shop. "We met a few private orders for it, sir, but we won't be stocking the book and certainly wouldn't put it on display," a friend was told, and he was made to feel that even mentioning the matter put him in the position of a man wearing wellington-boots at a St. Clare's party. [St. Clare's is a girls' college situated in Oxford.] Blackwell's and their satellites cannot have the excuse that there isn't enough demand for Nabokov because they are able to take what ought to be the suicidal risk of laying in large stocks of (e.g.) Snow's juvenilia and G. B. Stern, and if the policy on "Lolita" is deliberate, it amounts to a censorship.

According to the *Daily Express*, the duenna, being, among other things, sensitive about her influence (as the reference to the "satellites" suggests, Blackwell's now has an interest in many other Oxford bookshops), forbade the editors of *Isis* ever to mention Blackwell's name again in the pages of the magazine. This report touched off a row in the national press, whereupon a Blackwell's representative smugly assured a reporter from a London newspaper that "Lolita" was "a loathsome, morbid book." The reporter asked Sir Basil if the bookshop would sell *him* a copy. "I shall scrutinize you very carefully first," Sir Basil answered. "I don't think young people are much interested in this sort of thing. It's middle-aged men I'm wary of selling it to."

The dons, too, were outraged. In their own university journal, the *Oxford Magazine*, an anonymous tutor of poetic bent wrote:

> Blackwell's must not have a mention—
> Like the Holy Name of old—
> Or Sir Basil's legal henchmen,
> Virtue's knight, for right enrolled,
> Will drag away to dire detention
> Editors so basely bold.

Who are they that they should question
Orders of that learned knight,
Or hesitate the least suggestion
That he has not judged aright.

Let the Isis roll in silence;
Cherwell's waters have the right
To sing with tumbling genuflections
"Blackwell's are a source of light."

I was an undergraduate at Oxford just before the "Lolita" fracas, and although I had been buying most of my books at Blackwell's since I went up to the university, and have continued to do so, I have mixed feelings about the shop. Its fame may be deserved, and yet I remember it as a fierce place. The corner in which to sit and read a book through and the space in which to browse were both luxuries of an age long past; now students and dons, landladies and tourists jostle one another on the floor as though they were snatching a last drink before the pub closed. Also, the past afforded at least a score of alternatives to buying at Blackwell's, but today one would be hard put to it to find two or three genuine rivals. Blackwell's impersonality no doubt arises largely from its size (in a year it sells about two million books, for as many pounds [now three million books for twice as many pounds]), its top-heavy mail-order business (with the help of seasonal catalogues on about thirty-five subjects, it receives ninety per cent of its income from sales to customers writing in for books), and its terrifying efficiency (though it receives announcements of forthcoming books no sooner than any other bookshop, it almost invariably manages to beat everyone in including new books in its catalogues), but, whatever the reasons, and whatever the exigencies of being a bookseller in a time like the present, the fact remains that a bookshop that functions much as Sears, Roebuck does may arouse admiration, and even respect, but has difficulty inspiring affection. Perhaps because of this, some undergraduates sent up a restrained cheer when the near-monopoly of the Oxford book market held by Blackwell's and its "satellites" was challenged—after I went down from Oxford—by a new bookshop with about ten thousand square feet of floor space and complete with, among other things, coffee bar, record and music shop, and display of small scientific instruments and machines and stuffed birds, all housed behind plate glass in a modern building situated, unnervingly, just across the Magdalen Bridge. A few of them even conjectured that Robert Maxwell, the proprietor of this chic establishment, might be the shade of the original Benjamin Harris Blackwell in modern dress.

I had always taken it for granted that Sir Basil, who is seventy-five, would be as fierce as the enterprise he chairs, but when I said as much to an Oxford friend visiting me in America, where I was living at the time, he replied, "Who, the old Baz? On the contrary. I agree, one expects him to be a strong-armed gent, but, with that hope which springs eternal in the human breast, one secretly wishes that such a bookseller would turn out to be something cozy and soft. Well, he is. He runs his firm like a paterfamilias, with nineteenth-century principles of paternalism perpetually in mind. Oh, I don't mean to say that he's not a businessman, but he's also something of a gentle soul. If you can't pay your bills, the book-shop overlooks the delinquency—except, that is, for half a dozen reminders—for a year or so. Then begins a three-year cycle of dunning letters. The last dunning is the most serious, but when it comes, if you're up to it, you march into the shop and demand to see the Sir. Upstairs in his office, you shed a few tears, and the Sir will start the cycle of bills and dunning letters over again."

Recently, finding myself in England, I wrote to Sir Basil—or Gaffer, as he makes a point of insisting that he be called—asking if I might have a talk with him about the way serious bookselling is done, and then I went around to his establishment one Saturday morning at the bleary hour of seven-fifteen, the time of my appointment. The main door, in the eighteenth-century façade —which was as narrow and small as the shop behind it was sprawling and huge—was bolted, but I found my way in through a side driveway, in which vans were being loaded with big bags of books. In the shop, the air smelled of glue, paper, and wood, but if it seemed at first a little musty and close, it was pleasant once one got used to breathing it. A studious contingent of timid girls still in their teens, who seemed all stockings and stiletto heels, and of careworn men dressed in tweed coats were silently dusting and arranging books and going over cash-register receipts. I asked the way to Sir Basil's office, and was shown up to a room at the head of one of the Queen Anne staircases. The office was small and uncarpeted, and a little chilly, but its window afforded one of Ox-ford's loveliest views—across to the Sheldonian Theatre and down the road to the new Bodleian Library. Sir Basil, a spare but heavy-boned man with a certain amount of white hair and an innocent pink face beginning to be creased by age but lighted up by a cherubic smile, was perched on the edge of a desk that was empty except for neat bundles of envelopes tied with string. He was wearing a light-gray three-piece suit, a white shirt, and a pink shantung tie. He came across as soft, gray, and bumbling.

At a word from Sir Basil, I took a chair beside the desk. An instant later, he called out "Kay, will you come and help the Gaffer?" and began cutting open the bundles of letters on his desk.

A slender girl in her teens with grave gray eyes and wearing high heels tiptoed in from an adjoining room, and smiled shyly at Sir Basil.

"This is my honorary granddaughter," he told me. "One of the nice things about being old is that you can have innocent tender feelings for young girls. She never misses a Saturday—do you, Kay? I have at least a hundred sweet young things—frippets—but she's my favorite. I'm looking for Prince Charming for her, aren't I, Kay?"

"If you say so, Gaffer," Kay replied, taking up a position at a machine, at one end of the desk, that slit open the envelopes and piled them up in a tray.

I asked Sir Basil if he was always at work so early.

"Yes," he replied, and he added, like a minister quoting chapter and verse, "My father used to say, 'A day's work must be done in a day.' " Observing that the postman was by no means as punctual as he and Kay were, he continued, "If the postman isn't here when we arrive, I ring the post office every three minutes. One day, the postmaster rang *me*. He said they were stopping the second pickup on Saturday. I asked, 'Suppose we deliver our book bags'—we have made special arrangements for sending sixty-five-pound bags of books overseas—'to your Broad Street branch, will you have to send them out that day?' The postmaster said, 'Every last piece of post has to be sent out from every branch every day.' 'Thank you. That's good,' I said. On the following Saturday, I had one of our vans filled up with book bags and sent them around to the Broad Street post office. The postal clerk looked horrified, and immediately rang through to the head office for an auxiliary postal van. But no sooner had their van arrived than another of our vans pulled up with more book bags. I also filled up every postbox in the vicinity with our outgoing letters. No private person here could post a letter that Saturday. I waited for the postmaster's call. He rang through on Monday and curtly said, 'There will be a second pickup on Saturday.' "

Sir Basil went on talking as he looked through his mail. "I always get up at five-thirty—a routine I got into during the war, when I took in evacuees and relatives to live in my house, a few miles southwest of here," he said. "It's in Appleton Osse Field, in north Berkshire. Appleton Osse Field extends for a mile, from the Village Cross to Appleton Common, and is bounded by Osse Dyke. Because of a pedantic quirk of mine, the house has no name, but it is *in* Appleton Osse Field. When I get up, I put on my business suit—it keeps the bed warmth in—

and go straight downstairs to my library and curl up
with a rug on the sofa and read a book for a while. Then
I run out to my hut—a summerhouse—and leave my suit
there and take a cold swim in my pool. In weather fair or
foul, I always have a dip in the morning. Originally, the
pool was just part of Osse Dyke Brook that I had enlarged for myself, and every morning I went there and
took a swim, but after the war, when the state reim-
bursed me for what are called Post-War Credits, I piped
water in from the city. After a swim, in fair weather, I
sit naked on the green and contemplate nature, and then
I start my exercises, prescribed in 'My System,' by J. P.
Muller, who is one splendid man. I should do twelve
rounds of certain drills, but I do only three rounds now.
I bend down and touch my toes and tilt myself like a
windmill, and then make myself into a seesaw." He
jumped to his feet and put on a demonstration. "After
I do these exercises three times," he said, sitting down
again, "all my muscles are stretched and cleared of grit,
and I put on my suit and come inside and cook myself
breakfast. My good wife, the Mimi, used to help me
cook breakfast, but it didn't seem right to make her rise
from bed so early, so I do it myself. For this, she gives
me pocket money of a pound a week. I drive in to the
office and am here at eight-fifteen or eight-thirty, except
for Saturday, when I'm here at seven-fifteen. I usually
arrive with the post, which comes in from virtually
every country served by the Postal Union. Most of my
morning is taken up with the post. We get anywhere
from fifteen hundred to two thousand pieces of mail a
day, and I look at all of them. I personally answer such

complaints as we get, because I've developed the art of writing a letter that rarely fails to bring back a letter of apology. It means something for people to receive a letter from the chairman of the firm, and I always take the blame for the mistake and say we are all human together. Usually, I get a letter back going something like this: 'Dear Sir Basil, I wrote my letter in a fit of bad temper. . . .' "

Sir Basil laughed. All the time he had been talking, he had been flipping through envelopes, glancing at post-cards, discarding advertisements in windowed envelopes, and separating the airmail envelopes from the rest. He made a pile of orders for books for Kay to stamp and route to the proper sections of the bookshop and the accounts department, and he set aside the letters of com-plaint to answer later. "Some people write in because they are indignant at the quality of our service, and others because they've received a dunning—though I must hasten to add we have remarkably few bad debts," he said. "I've often thought of inventing a dialogue between Socrates and a friend, and putting it on our letterhead. 'Socrates,' the friend would ask, 'what would you say is the test of a reasonable and good man?' Socra-tes would answer, 'A man who can be gentlemanly when he is asked to pay his bills.' " [In recent years, the following has actually appeared at the foot of Black-well's dunning letter: "How then, Socrates, shall we recognise the truly just and generous man? It is he who, being reminded of an obligation, is able gracefully to thank his creditor for prompting him to do his duty. PLATO, Dial. Frag. Apoc." This "apocryphal" source has apparently never been challenged by any of Black-well's debtors.] Sir Basil paused to savor the effect of his words, and then went on, under his breath, "Here is a pretty Taiwan . . . a Bhutan . . . a Seychelles . . . a Luangprabang. Every morning, I put the pretty foreign stamps here"—he banged the left corner of his desk several times—"but at some point during the time Kay is helping me mince and sort the post, the stamps disappear."

Kay smiled, and Sir Basil turned to the letters of complaint—or "growls," as I discovered he usually called them. In the course of the morning, I came to realize he had a whimsical term for everything. "Here is a gr-rowl from Mr. Ed-wards of Scot-land," he said. "His grievance is that he came into the shop and bought books worth more than sixteen pounds and yet was charged postage. On orders much smaller than his, Blackwell's pays the postage. On top of that, he says the books were badly packed."

At Sir Basil's elbow was a Telemat—a receiverless telephone with rows of buttons, a dial, a small speaker, and a mouthpiece. He dialled a number and was immediately answered by a thin, efficient voice.

"Are you the shepherdess who looks after the flock of 'E's?" Sir Basil asked.

"Yes, sir."

"Shepherdess, how many do you have in your flock?"

"Six thousand, sir."

"Well, my dear, would you be so good as to look and see if Mr. Edwards, from Aberdeen, was sent some books?"

"Yes, sir."

"Thank you."

Sir Basil dialled another number.

"Yes, sir," a man's voice answered.

"My dear man, would you check and see who packed the books for Receipt Number 617,432?"

Within a few moments, a boy came scampering up to Sir Basil's office, full of apologies. Handing over the receipt to Sir Basil, he said that he was the culprit who had packed the books for Mr. Edwards, and that he had charged him for postage by mistake.

"It will never happen again, will it, my man?" Sir Basil asked.

"Never, Gaffer," the boy said.

"That's good," Sir Basil said.

Sir Basil dismissed the boy and dialled back the clerk in charge of the "E"s. He asked her to call off the search for Edwards, since by tracking down the receipt he had learned that Mr. Edwards had paid cash, so no invoice had been necessary. He shouted "Miss Halliday!" and then took time to explain to me that this was Miss Eleanor Halliday, a lady of "great probity" who had been working for him as his secretary for thirty-four years, always keeping the same hours he did—seven-fifteen or eight-fifteen to five, with a break for a sandwich, or "nosebag." In private life, he added, she was the happy wife of one Major Atkinson.

Miss Halliday, a solid-looking lady of medium height with graying hair, entered, and Sir Basil dictated to her a letter for Mr. Edwards: "I am replying personally to your letter of July 3rd to express my dismay that your parcel was inadequately packed. It is a most unusual occurrence, and I think it must have been the work of an enthusiastic but inexperienced youth. Happily, the books were not damaged. The young man who served you apologizes for adding the cost of postage. He said he knew better, and will do better next time. I enclose a Postal Order for 6d., and promise you that your parcels will be well packed in future. Yours sincerely . . ." Later, when the secretary brought him the typed letter, he signed it.

Picking up another letter from his desk and reading it to himself, Sir Basil said, "Dear, dear, here is a gremlin," and he explained to me, "That means getting more than one complaint from the same person." He went on, "The correspondent complains that she ordered two copies of a book, one to be sent to her, the other to a friend in the hospital, but *both* turned up on her doorstep. She sent us a throaty growl, but to no avail, for a few days later she ordered a copy of another book with instructions that it should await the recipient's name and address—the book was to be a gift—and it, too, turned up on her doorstep." Sir Basil asked Miss Halliday to put aside the letter until he could look through the lady's complete file—his usual procedure with a "gremlin."

Having looked at the next letter, Sir Basil said, "Master Jonathan James, of Sedley School, in Cambridge, attacks us on our publishing side. He writes, 'Dear Basil Blackwell, In your animal book you have made a big mistake the camel has *two* humps and the dromedary *one* hump please excuse me writing to you about it. Jonathan James.' "

Sir Basil sent Kay for the dictionary and the animal book, and, with both books open in front of him, he dictated an answer: "Dear Jonathan James, I am writing to thank you for your letter, in which you tell me that we have made a mistake in our animal book. I am not quite sure that we have. My dictionary tells me that a dromedary is a 'light, fleet, usually Arabian or one-humped camel,' called a dromedary because it runs. 'Dromas' is a Greek word for 'runner.' The dictionary also tells me that the camel is a 'large, hornless, ruminant, long-necked, cushion-footed quadruped,' with one hump if it is an Arabian camel and two humps if it is a Bactrian camel. I think, then, that the photograph on page 14 of the 'Wild Animals' book must be a dromedary, or one-humped Arabian camel, and that is what we should have said about it. Thank you for cleverly spotting this point. May I show my gratitude by enclosing a little Book Token? Yours sincerely . . ."

A poodle had been bouncing around the room for some time, and now Sir Basil took notice of it. "That's Ricky, who belongs to our children's shop," he told me. "Originally, the shop was a department here, and the children used to sit and read; we had to be very careful not to step on them, because they always sat with their legs outstretched. When things got too crowded, my son Richard suggested that we take over a separate shop for children. I was against banishing them from here, but the new children's shop, in a small, poky three-story house right across from Balliol, is a great success. There we have built seats for children, but they still prefer to sit on the floor to read books. We try to have books for all children, from tiny tots to boys and girls of fifteen and sixteen, though often when they're sixteen, especially if they're boys, we have some difficulty in helping them, because they get interested nowadays in those horrible technical books."

While Sir Basil sorted and read and dictated letters, a bevy of girls flew in and out of his room doing his bidding—carrying a bundle of orders to the theology department, or helping him and Kay dispose of other mail.

"I don't think I've seen you before," he said to one brunette.

"I started only yesterday, sir," she replied.

"Can you type?"

"No, sir," she said. "I'm going to learn it here."

"Those are wicked winkle-pickers you have on," he said, eying her high heels. Turning to me, he continued, "Have you noticed that sometimes these girls are three inches higher and sometimes three inches lower? It's because of these winkle-pickers."

The girl laughed.

"You know, each time these frippets take a step, they put *eight hundred pounds* of pressure on a square inch, or so someone told me," Sir Basil went on. "I know it's hard on their feet, but it's even harder on my linoleum."

Two girls entered silently and went over to help Kay.

"Are you both new?" Sir Basil asked.

"Yes, sir," they replied in unison.

"Don't tell me your names, because I won't remember them, but tell me how long you have been here," he said.

"Four months, sir," one said.

"Four weeks, sir," the other said.

"Now that we have a staff of nearly five hundred, it is very difficult to know everyone's name," Sir Basil said to me. "When we had only sixty or seventy employees, I knew everything about everyone." He turned to the girls. "Are you diligent girls?"

Both the girls looked blank.

"You don't know what 'diligent' means?"

"No, sir."

"Well, 'diligent' means 'working hard.'"

"Yes, sir."

"I've always had a passion for my frippets," he said to me. "My wife often gives me carnations, and I bring them in and hand them around. The frippets put them in their hair. Kay, last night I gave you four roses—one for you, one for your sister, and two for your mother. Did you do as I bade?"

"Yes, Gaffer," she said.

He held out his hand to her with a few coins in it and said, "Would you pick some money and, when you're finished here, buy Gee's Linctus for the Mimi? Do you know what Gee's Linctus is?"

"Yes, Gaffer." Kay picked out two half crowns from his hand and put them aside on the desk.

"The Mimi has come down with a bad throat, and, remember, she has to be in good condition for tea tomorrow," Sir Basil said, and he went on, to me, "I often have my Cinderellas for tea. It is a great occasion. They pick daffodils, you see. So many of the Oxford girls are beat. Their hair is not combed, their necks and ears are dirty. But my frippets are nice, fresh things. I suppose that's really why I like them. I like to look at a beautiful, clean, healthy face."

He said that most of his girls were recruited, with the help of their headmistresses, at sixteen, as they were leaving central schools or one of the other institutions in Oxford. But no sooner had a frippet got the hang of things at Blackwell's than she got married. A girl would work at Blackwell's for about two years, go off and have a baby, come back for a while, and depart for good. Then the baby would grow up and come to work there. But times were changing. The girls, like the male clerks—his word for *them* was "archimandrites"—were very conscientious as long as they stayed, but Blackwell's was coming to be looked upon more and more as just a place for a job. The dedication and complete loyalty to the firm that were common in his father's day and his own earlier days were going. He did, however, always try to keep in touch with former staff members by giving a Christmas party each year for their children—his "grandchildren." The head of his publicity department, Mrs. Gladys Neale, kept a list of them, and it was part of her regular job to find out what each child wanted that cost less than a pound, buy it, wrap it, and have it ready for Sir Basil to hand out at the party. On Christmas Eve, he gave another party, for every last member of his working staff. It was traditionally held in the assembly hall at Carfax, and when it ended, he shook the hand of everyone, from director to office boy, each time with a fresh pound note in his hand. Everyone could use a pound note, he explained, but, more important, the gesture had the effect of putting all the members of his staff on a basis of equality as his children. In addition, any of his children who had not missed a day of work through illness during the year received a fiver, as part of what Sir Basil called his "health marathon."

"I say, here is a rather nice one!" Sir Basil exclaimed, turning up another letter. It was from C. E. Stevens, the tutor of ancient history at Magdalen College, he said, and he went on to read it aloud: " 'Dear Sir Basil, The reason for answering a Christmas card in weather only appropriate for Christmas in Australia is not, I am happy to say, that I am full of guilt and shame with a large bill to the Store. It is the more humiliating one of just having neglected to do my duty. May I take this very belated opportunity of wishing you this and many more years of happiness and prosperity to the Shop. It is exactly thirty years since Blackwell's first presented an account to me at this address. The firm has got my books and suffered my credit for a long time now. I think tenderly of the Shop and of the man whose name it bears.' " Sir Basil thumped his desk jubilantly. "Isn't that nice!" he shouted.

I asked Sir Basil if he was able to deal with all his correspondence as easily as he had with that morning's letters.

"Yes—unless the writer happens to be George Bernard Shaw," he said.

He had at hand a pamphlet containing a record of a bout with Shaw—the page containing the exchange was headed "SNOWS OF YESTERYEAR . . . *Members may like to be reminded of former glories*"—which he now exhibited more in the spirit of a conqueror than in that of a man who had been vanquished in battle.

An opening letter from Sir Basil read:

DEAR MR. SHAW,

When Constable and Co. published "The Complete Plays of Bernard Shaw" at 12s. 6d. net, they assured the Trade that there would be no reprint. This statement was freely used by booksellers in selling the book to their customers.

The publication of "The Complete Plays of Bernard Shaw" by Odhams Press for sale solely to subscribers to the *Daily Herald* (at 3s. 9d. plus six tokens) has placed those booksellers in the unfortunate position of having deceived the public.

It must be admitted that the new edition differs from the "Complete Edition" in containing three more plays (though this is small consolation to the original purchasers!); but apart from these extra pages and the Warning from the author, apparently the new edition is in fact a reprint from the plates of Constable's edition.

I can hardly suppose that Constable gave the booksellers their assurance without your consent. It would help those booksellers (already sufficiently penalised) who are charged by their customers with a breach of faith, if you could arm them with a statement exonerating them from complicity.

Yours sincerely . . .

To Blackwell's bumbling, Shaw responded like a hornet:

DEAR BASIL BLACKWELL,

In future, when a customer asks you for a book of mine, say "Thanks very much," wrap the book up nicely in paper for him (or her), take the money, give the change, say "Thanks very much" over again, and bow the customer out.

If, out of pure gratuitous incontinence, you prefer to enter into conversation and give unsolicited assurances, of an obviously idiotic character, about my business intentions, you do it at your own risk; and if it turns out subsequently that I never had any such intentions, you will have to exonerate yourself as best you can.

I have given Constable's a letter to the effect that they took no part in the *Daily Herald* transaction, except to oppose it with all their might. I can do nothing for the booksellers but tell them not to be childish.

In America, I have lately had two orders of 50,000 copies each from book clubs, to be given away to their members *for nothing*, as a bonus. Of course, I accepted both.

I am looking forward to an order from Woolworth's for a sixpenny edition.

Would you, Basil, refuse such business, if it came your way?

And have you no bowels of compassion for the millions of your fellow countrymen who can no more afford a twelve-and-sixpenny book than a trip round the world? You should see some of their letters.

I am really surprised at you. When we met at Bumpus's, you seemed quite an intelligent youth.

> Faithfully . . .

Sir Basil asked if I would enjoy visiting the room where he was born, which was now the office of his son Richard. I said yes, and he led the way up the second flight of the Queen Anne staircase, singing loudly a full chorus of "Hole in the Bucket." "You know," he said as we reached the landing, "when the bookshop was small, there was a wonderful tradition of all the assistants' breaking into song, but now, except for the old man, no one sings. I open the church festivities in Appleton every New Year with this song. Last year, the Mimi threatened to bite my leg off if I did it again, but I don't think I'll ever be able to give it up."

We had been hovering outside a door on the landing, and now Sir Basil knocked on the door and opened it. There was no one in the room. "Richard said he was coming in today, though usually I'm the only director here on Saturday," he said. "Richard had an admirable education for building character. He went to Winchester, and no school has ever had more effect on a boy. He liked it from the first day, and before he left he was the president of the Boat Club. At Oxford, he rowed in his college eights and did brilliantly in classics. How do you like my manger?"

The office we were standing in had no resemblance to a manger—or, indeed, to Sir Basil's den downstairs. There was a carpet on the floor, and the desk was piled high with bundles of papers, folders, and memorandum pads; the emanation was unmistakably that of a business executive. "You see, the world revolves around Richard now," Sir Basil said. "The day-to-day administration has passed into his hands. I'm just tolerated as an old man in residence. Richard belongs to the new generation. My greatest concern in life has been not to get in the way of my sons. A lot of fathers overshadow their sons and don't let them flower, but I want my sons to be better than their father. Richard is a very daring boy; he's taking a good, hard look at a proposal to put a computer in the bookshop."

A restless-looking pear-shaped man in his early forties stepped into the room. He was Richard Blackwell. "Gaffer, three tourists are waiting to see you downstairs," he announced.

"Oh dear, it's time for me to give my audience," Sir Basil said. He explained that each Saturday morning he set aside an hour or two for receiving visitors, listening to complaints, and hearing reasons someone should be given a reprieve from dunning. He pattered off down the stairs.

Young Blackwell took a swivel chair and immediately started talking—first about the modern era and then about the family arrangements for the future of the bookshop. Once upon a time, he said, all the Oxford tradesmen—the tailors, the wine merchants, the goldsmiths and silversmiths—had done business almost exclusively with the students and the university, extending unlimited credit and giving a very personal type of service. Today, the clients of the Oxford tradesmen were the steelworkers at Cowley; in fact, they hardly ever saw an undergraduate. Blackwell's, in doing a large business with the gown, was an exception, but even Blackwell's would eventually have to come to terms with the new times. Sir Basil, having seen the signs, now left the policy decisions more and more up to him and his younger brother, Julian. Sir Basil had already divided up his assets. He had given the freehold part of the bookshop—about twenty-five hundred square feet of ground area—to him, and was leaving the house in Appleton Osse Field to Julian. Alas, his grandfather had made a bad mistake in missing an opportunity to acquire the freehold to the rest of the bookshop from Trinity. Sir Basil had, however, managed to keep on very good terms with the college, and had foresightedly sent Julian there; Blackwell's had just received permission to build an annex on Trinity property behind the bookshop.

The Telemat buzzed in young Blackwell's office, and Sir Basil's good-humored voice came over the loudspeaker. He had adjourned his audience and wished me to rejoin him in his office. As I was leaving Richard Blackwell, he said, "My father is a rare spirit, but he needs somewhat grosser spirits to look after him and keep his feet planted on the ground."

I found Sir Basil chuckling over some mimeographed sheets, which he said were "a newspaper partly written and edited by myself." He went on to tell me that it was put out monthly for the members of the "Blackwell's society" and was called the *Broad Sheet*. "Here are some choice items," he said, and he added, under his breath, "Some more of the Gaffer's prose."

The choice items read:

Apart from being unattractive and bad for you, stiletto heels do a great deal of damage to our floor coverings. If you cannot wear flat shoes at work, which is much the most sensible thing to do, then buy some plastic caps for your heels, and save our floors if not yourselves. . . .

We regret the water heater for the top floor cloakroom is so often out of action; someone must have cursed this heater from the moment it was installed. It now leaks; a plumber was sent for, but he referred us to the Gas Company. We wait their verdict; we are told this infernal machine needs a new diaphragm. . . . The geyser is there, but not connected. If one turns the tap, at the moment, the water rushes to the ceiling and floods everything. . . .

The Archbishop of Canterbury's pamphlet in reply to "Honest to God" was equally sold out in two days. Our 200 copies went in that time, and like all the rest it is now reprinting. We were concerned for the clergyman who ordered—in this order—"Honest to God," "Objections," "God Is No More," and "The Good-Food Guide." We felt he was giving up the unequal struggle. To the aggressive lady who demanded loudly "Have you any 'Objections to Christianity'?" one was very tempted to reply "None at all, Madam." . . .

April has been a good month for New Libraries . . . and the first order has been received from the University of East Anglia. The University of Ife (Ibadan branch) have added 46 titles to their subscription list, and Rutherford College of Further Education–22. . . . Standard Telecommunication Laboratories, Ltd., have sent us a list of 450 periodicals and asked us to quote [prices]. . . .

Congratulations to John Wraight and Michael Honour on the apprehension of 2 malefactors [book thieves].

Sir Basil remarked that Blackwell's was a sort of society of men contributing to the cause of learning, even if they only packed books, transcribed addresses and records, or placed books on the shelves. The main qualification for a shop assistant was a good memory—the ability to recall quickly the author, title, and publisher of a book—for he thereby saved himself laborious research, saved his employers overhead costs, and saved his customers time. This sort of good memory, for the most part, was acquired by apprentices from an older generation of archimandrites. During the Second World War, though, an older generation of archimandrites had passed from the scene without ever having a chance to train a new one, and now it looked as though there might not be any generation to train, for boys leaving school found an easier and brighter future waiting for them in the steel mills. Perhaps the hope of good bookselling now lay in an occasional clever boy who messed up his university career and took to the life simply because he wished to deal with books on any footing.

"What say we look in on the Mimi for a bite in Appleton Osse Field this evening and carry on talking over some scoff?" Sir Basil said. "She's expecting you for the weekend."

Sir Basil's house turned out to be modest in scale in that it was set in about seven acres of land, but those seven acres were complete with meadow, kitchen garden, orchard of two hundred and fifty apple trees, and garden of seven hundred and fifty rose bushes. Sir Basil had driven me out from Oxford, and as we pulled up he said, "You are about to meet the nicest woman in the world, the Mimi. I have been married to her for half a century." Entering the house, he made the walls shake by shouting "*Home!*" and then he explained, with a laugh, "My way of telling the Mimi the Master is home." Again he bellowed "*Home!*" and this time he added, "Mimi, the Gaffer is come!"

"Gaf-fer, I am in earshot," a meticulous voice answered from upstairs. "Don't deaf-en the Mi-mi." Then Lady Blackwell started coming down the stairs. She had broad shoulders, and mouse-colored hair turning white, which curled softly around her face. She was wearing a plain blue cotton dress, which emphasized the color of her eyes. Her bearing was a little severe, with something of the schoolmistress about it; she looked very country and very competent. At the foot of the stairs, she kissed Sir Basil, greeted me, and turned back to Sir Basil, saying, "Please show the guest to his room. I will be pottering about in the kitchen for some time yet."

"What the pussycat orders, so does the Gaffer," Sir Basil said, and he led the way upstairs.

The house was furnished, for the most part, with unpolished oak tables and chairs, and had the look of a rambling cottage. After a wash in my room, I rejoined Sir Basil, who was sitting on the lawn in a deck chair reading a copy of the *Daily Telegraph*. "You can have a soak later," he said—I had already discovered that "soak" and "nip" were his words for a drink—"but first come and take a turn with me in the garden."

It was twilight. The roses were well tended, and the turf between the beds was well cropped. The apples rotting on the ground—picking them was too expensive, Sir Basil explained, and they were waiting for a part-time gardener to bury them—somehow looked as though they had been strewn there deliberately. There was also a brook filled with trout, not far from Sir Basil's swimming pool. We passed pieces of garden sculpture strategically placed here and there, including an elf standing in the middle of a pond and holding up a fish.

In the distance, church bells began to peal. "Oho! That is Cuthbert White," Sir Basil exclaimed, and he added that the Whites had been the village bell ringers for a hundred and twenty years. "Once, I had a religious experience," he continued after we'd taken a few turns around the garden. "It had to do with a fever of anti-Semitism I suffered from. One day in 1944, a Dominican monk came by the bookshop; he stopped in at my office, and I told him about my anti-Semitism and how it troubled me. I asked him if he would put in a word for me. He must have said a prayer for me the very same evening, because I woke up the next morning and the anti-Semitism was gone. It had fallen off me like the pack from Christian's back."

I asked him if he thought that Fascist propaganda had had anything to do with the onset of his anti-Semitism.

"No, I don't think so," Sir Basil replied. "It had to do, I suppose, with one of my daughters marrying a half-Jew. Actually, one night in 1939 I was lying in the bathtub and I suddenly got the idea that Mussolini and Hitler were not only telling lies but also drawing false conclusions *from* their lies. Then it came to me that the only way to combat them was by an appeal to the essence of Christianity—by having the Pope or some other Christian leader take charge of broadcasting stations throughout the world and recite the Lord's Prayer to this worldwide audience. But before I could put this idea to the Vatican or to Canterbury, Germany had attacked Poland."

I asked Sir Basil how he had become interested in religious matters.

"When I was a young man, and especially at the time I was reading Greats, I went through a period of skepticism," he said. "I found my way back to God when, one day, I woke up with the need to say 'Thank you.' Once I'd started saying 'Thank you,' I felt the need to ask forgiveness, and in order to do that, I had to believe in someone. I became very religious. For many years, I was Appleton's churchwarden. Then I gave that up, because I discovered that I was singing hymns and psalms that were nonsense. Now I go to church only for the form of it; I like the formality of the service. Tomorrow I am going to have a long lie-in, because there is no Communion service. I usually go to the Communion service at eight o'clock, but one Sunday a month they don't have the Communion service but only the sickly Matins service at nine-thirty. I often wish I were a Catholic. The Catholics do the best job of solving the puzzle. Of course, it still remains a puzzle, but they have one foot on the other side. I think it is more difficult to live a life of virtue out in the world than behind the gates of a monastery.

The Trappists and the Carthusians have it very easy. It's much more difficult to love virtue with the temptations of the world all around you—temptations to be proud, to be greedy, to be avaricious."

It was getting chilly, and we went inside. We found Lady Blackwell stoking a fire in the library—a room lined with a reader's books rather than a collector's.

Sitting down in front of the fire, Sir Basil said, "Once, when I went to a flick—I don't often—one of the men in it said that there wasn't a day in his life when he wouldn't have remarried his wife. I feel the same about the Mimi. It's not original, but it's true."

"Now, Gaffer, if you aren't careful, you'll tell the guest the date of our golden wedding anniversary," Lady Blackwell said. Turning to me, she explained, "We don't want to see our picture in the paper holding each other's hands and laughing. Such pictures of old people always make me uncomfortable."

Sir Basil offered me a "nip," and poured me a glass of sherry at a side table. He and Lady Blackwell each took a glass of water, informing me that they were both secret teetotallers, taking only an occasional glass of wine.

"You know, a very nice thing happened to me today," Sir Basil said when he had sat down again. "Wilson Knight, the Shakespeare critic, came by the office. Visits from men like him are a rather nice part of bookselling. I told Knight something about Shakespeare *he* didn't know."

"What did you tell him, Gaffer?" Lady Blackwell asked.

"That in the original version of 'Hamlet' the Ghost

said nothing. He just appeared and beckoned to Hamlet, and Hamlet spent a little time with him offstage. Since no one knew what the Ghost had told Hamlet, the motives of his subsequent actions remained a mystery. The play was far more interesting that way. It was the theatre manager who insisted that Shakespeare write a speech for the Ghost. The theatre manager said the audience was too dim to follow such an oblique treatment."

"And, pray, how do you know that, Basil?" Lady Blackwell asked.

"Exactly the same way the Catholics know that the Virgin Mary went to Heaven in the flesh—through the imagination."

"There you go again, Gaffer—inventing historical data when you know I like information," said Lady Blackwell. "I hope you told Mr. Knight that it was fantasy."

"I did," Sir Basil said, "and we had a good laugh."

The telephone rang, and Sir Basil went to answer it. When he returned, he said that it was Per Saugman, head of Blackwell's Scientific Publications, who had just bought for Blackwell's the best bookshop in Denmark—Munksgaard, of Copenhagen—thus extending Blackwell's interests overseas.

"Why did he have to disturb the prophet in his chamber?" Lady Blackwell asked.

"He's just spent a hundred thousand quid of my money," Sir Basil replied. "That's important." Turning to me, he continued, "Richard goes on the modern theory that one should borrow and expand, that money exists only on paper, that it can be created by adding a few noughts to a figure. But"—Sir Basil sighed—"when it comes to money, I think like a village grocer."

"Gaffer is such a village grocer about money that he won't draw out all of his year's salary," Lady Blackwell said. "He's afraid that the firm would collapse if he took out the whole seven thousand pounds."

"The children have been talking about installing a computer, but there's only one question I'd like to put to the computer," Sir Basil went on, as though he had rehearsed the question. "When will a firm that on the average gives three months of credit, buys on one month of credit, expands at the rate of fifteen per cent a year, and sacrifices fifty-two per cent of its annual profits to the income-tax collectors—when will it burst? No doubt the computer would burst before answering such a question." Sir Basil laughed.

"Now it's time for dinner," Lady Blackwell said.

As we walked into a long, bare dining room, furnished in heavy-looking unpolished oak, Sir Basil said, "You know, in Appleton we have a rather nice way of ringing the passing bell. They put a leather pad on one side of the clapper, and leave the other as it is, so that sharp and muffled sounds alternate. At the first thud, the villagers know that one of their number has died. I hope the custom will still be carried on when the Guardian Angel comes calling for me. But I hope that won't be very soon." He filled the room with a shout of laughter.

1964

1971. Sir Basil writes, "I have not changed my way of life in the last seven years, and the Mimi and I are still to be likened to the 'two bright and aged snakes' in

Matthew Arnold's poem. On my 80th birthday in '69 I promoted myself to the office of president of the firm, a condition resembling that of the Cheshire Cat in 'Alice in Wonderland,' who in his elevated position began to fade out 'beginning with the end of the tail and ending with the grin.' Those Blackwellians whom you met are still mainly with us; but for me there is a disastrous gap. My peerless Secretary, Eleanor, after thirty-seven years of infallible service and perfect health, was stricken by lung cancer (cigarettes were her only frailty) in November, '67, and died painfully, but undaunted, in the following July, taking with her half my business memory and no little of my joy in the day's work. She cannot be replaced. Richard's two boys, Miles and Nigel, are now Blackwellians, and Kay, grown to lovely womanhood and blissfully married, is now a pillar of our English Literature department. Physically at Blackwell's there has been a startling development. Trinity College set about building a new quadrangle, and we through the initiative of son Julian planned a vast room beneath it, with a range of 10,000 square feet and shelves offering to the view some 170,000 volumes. As our civilisation shows more and more the tendency to disintegrate—to make way perhaps for a new and better order?—so the more confidently I look to books, which reveal the wisdom and follies of ages past, to be our guides in years to come."

IV

There Is No Telling

In 1964, AN EDITORIAL COMMENT APPEARING IN *The New Yorker* applauded the bequest of half a million dollars made by Mr. Ataullah K. Ozai-Durrani—the inventor of Minute Rice—for financing the translation into English of the works of two Urdu poets, Mirza Asadullah Khan Ghalib and Mir Taqi Mir, and also the writing of their biographies. "There is no telling," the comment quixotically noted. "They may be terrible poets." In trying to come to terms with this unsettling suggestion, I was reminded of Mr. Hussein, one of my father's closest friends in Rawalpindi. I met him when I was about ten, and I remember him as a tall Pathan who appeared even taller because he always wore a turban tied high on his head. He was never seen without it, and we children believed that he wore it to bed. I don't recall his ever discussing any subject without sooner or later touching on Mir and Ghalib. He often observed that the younger generation was so uneducated in its own language and literature that it might as well be illiterate, noting that if one knew Urdu literature there was no reason to know any other, for Mir and Ghalib were better than Chaucer and Byron. He insisted that Mir and Ghalib were so great that any attempt at paraphrase or translation was defamatory. I also remember, however, that in expounding the Urdu poetry Mr. Hussein used to refer us to an English book, "A History of Urdu Literature," written by Ram Babu Saksena and published in Allahabad in 1927. I recently obtained a copy of this book, and have come to realize that Saksena effortlessly and naturally catches a flavor of the poets that might take anyone trained in the West years of unlearning to achieve.

Saksena tells us that Mir Mahommad Taqi, who signed himself Mir, lived from 1125 to 1223 A.H., or from 1793 to 1810 A.D. (Saksena uses both the Mohammedan lunar calendar and the Gregorian solar calendar, and this procedure gets him into difficulties, since by the first reckoning Mir died at the age of ninety-five and by the second at the age of seventeen; literary histories give his dates as 1722–1810 A.D.), and that his period "is one of great glory for Urdu poetry when it blossoms forth with a dazzling magnificence." He continues, "They [Mir and his contemporary Mirza Rafiuddin, whose pen name was Sauda] outshine their compeers in the beauty of their style, in the elegance and command of diction, in the mastery of technique, in the loftiness of thought, and in the delicacy of sentiment. *Ghazal* and *Qasida* reached a very high level." A *ghazal*, Saksena explains, is an erotic or mystical ode of ten or twelve couplets, and a *qasida*, which is anywhere from twenty-five to a hundred and seventy couplets long, is a poem with an avowed intention, and the poem may be "a panegyric or a satire or it may be didactic, philosophical, or religious." Saksena dwells on Mir's period at some length:

Love themes were handled with a freshness and effect not to be found before. . . . The lines were more compact, and had a greater swing. There was little looseness about them. They had more vigour and poignancy and appealed better to the ear. Quaint and far-fetched . . . figures of speech began to make their appearance oftener than before, but not to such an extent as to mar the beauty and confound the meaning of verses. They are harmoniously woven and do not obtrude very prominently. . . . Not only were the poets of this period the originators of certain poetic forms in Urdu, but they handled them so cleverly that they laid down the lines for further improvement. Their treatment, however, was conventional, modelled strictly on the canons of Persian poetry. The language [Urdu] made great and rapid strides and acquired vigour, range and elasticity. . . . It [the period] saw the rise of some of the greatest masters of Urdu verse . . . some of the most distinguished and honoured on the bead-roll of Urdu literature.

Saksena is at his rhetorical best, however, in discussing Mir's poetry and its place in his period:

Urdu poetry is popularly regarded to be co-extensive with the Urdu *ghazal* and as Mir is pre-eminent as a *ghazal* writer he is naturally regarded to be the greatest of Urdu poets. . . . His verses are simple, eloquent, poignant, winged with pathos and pain. . . . In the ardour of passion, in the melody and music . . . his *ghazals* rank the best in Urdu literature. . . . His *ghazals* are the elixir of Urdu poetry. . . . Mir's position is un-equalled in the history of Urdu literature. He is popularly called Khuda-i-Sakhun or "God of Poetry."

Saksena makes a valiant attempt at critical comment:

It is incorrect to say that Mir never attempted the satire and the *qasida*. He tried and proved a failure, as his genius did not lie that way.

But then he gracefully cancels his criticism:

> Mir's despondent nature, retired habits, and brooding mind, self-absorbed and hypercritical, did not permit him to scour widely over the field of human nature. The narrow outlook of Mir was the outcome of his concentration and proud temper. He wooed his muse with all the fervour and intensity of an ardent lover. Such was his self-effacement and his self-extinction in work that he did not notice for seven whole years a garden over which his sitting room looked out. Such absorption to the exclusion of everything else must result in high artistic work in its own circumscribed domain.

When Saksena comes to discuss Ghalib, he surpasses his discussion of Mir. He says that Ghalib "fully opens his heart to his readers and sings of . . . 'the slings and arrows of outrageous fortune,' his illusive and ever-receding hopes . . . the thousand and one attachments and affections of life, its pomp and circumstance, its joys and its vexation." He continues, "The intense pathos of life, the heart-rending anguish of helpless suffering, the blank bewilderment of unbearable misery, the stern and inexorable shocks of sudden misfortune, the painful consciousness, in short, that 'life is a sad funeral procession with the laughter of gods in the background,' all this finds an echo in his verses." But this particular consciousness, Saksena says, is only one facet of Ghalib's work, for "the tragic gloom of Ghalib's odes is occasionally relieved by rays of dazzling light." He goes on to say, "The sunshine and joy are interspersed with despair and darkness. . . . Ghalib is a consummate artist and has an astonishing power and felicity of presentation of the visual picture." To illustrate what he means by "the visual picture," Saksena quotes, in English translation, from Ghalib himself: " 'Ah! Love, the joy of night, the pride of heart, the peace of sweet sleep, belong to him over whose arms thy locks are gently waving.' " Saksena comments on the echo of Shelley elsewhere. He concludes, "Ghalib's . . . art is truly superb and yet superbly true," only to cap this epigram with another: "Once again beauty is truth and truth beauty." Ghalib is also "Khuda-i-Sakhun."

Perhaps I ought to stop here and admit that I accept on faith Saksena's questionable facts—which he rides like the proverbial beggar riding his wish-horse—because I am in love with Saksena's lush prose. His voice has the accent of my Indian childhood, and it speaks to me over the barrier of years and critical sensibility. I even tend to identify myself with the poets as Saksena recounts their lives. "Mir . . . drank copiously of the gall of life," Saksena writes. "His is a tale of woe. . . . His verses bear the motto 'Abandon all hope ye that enter here.' " Saksena explains that Mir Taqi Mir was the son of Mir Abdullah, one of the nobles in Akbarabad (Agra); that Mir Abdullah died when Mir Taqi Mir was just a child, and the boy left Akbarabad when the Emperor Shah Alam was on the throne; that afterward the boy lived with his uncle Khan Arzu, who himself was a well-known Persian poet, and who proceeded to supervise the boy's education; that the uncle taught the nephew the art of writing poetry; that Mir received great popular acclaim ("His verses were on the lips of everybody. His *ghazals* were taken from city to city as valuable presents"); that, like most poets, he was impecunious; and that he was too proud—had a "supersensitive nature," which prevented him from courting the nobility of Delhi and receiving patronage. Saksena ends his survey characteristically: "Only a few scanty details which are authentic are available about Mir's life."

And Ghalib's life? He repudiated, Saksena says, "the pleasure garden view of paradise and the glowing pictures of the gratification of sense as humiliating and demoralising to the purity of high ideals." And Saksena continues:

> He writes, "We know what paradise is in reality but oh Ghalib! it is a fine idea to keep one's heart happy!" [Urdu poets often speak of themselves in the third person] and again "True worship is not evoked by the thought of wine and honey. Hurl down such a paradise into hell." Ghalib believed that the supreme misfortune, the real tragedy of life, is individual self-consciousness, because it sunders the individual from the cosmic consciousness. . . . He cries out, "After all, I have a heart of flesh and blood. It is not a stone or a brick-a-bat; why then should it not be moved by sorrow?" . . . The concentrated passion, the unreasoning simple fond hopefulness, the pathetic clinging to fast vanishing faith, the dread of impending calamity but not the full consciousness of it are beautifully mirrored in the couplet in which he says, "Ah, friend! Why are you so nervous in telling me of the disaster in the garden? Why should it be my nest on which the lightning fell yesterday?"

Elsewhere, Saksena observes that Mirza Asadullah Khan Ghalib, who was born in 1797, was "sprung from a noble Central Asian family of Turks of the Aibak clan which traced its descent through the Saljuk kings to Faridun in the misty and legendary past." Ghalib's childhood was tragic, and his education intensive but haphazard. He lost his father at an early age, like Mir, and later, when he was nine, he also lost the uncle to whose care he had been committed. Because his relatives were well connected, the boy was given a pension to carry on with his education. He was fortunate in having excellent tutors. He grew up to be a good correspondent, have a host of friends, and be generous with his time and money—he was kind to aspiring poets. He drank and gambled, and behaved like a grandee, and apologized in his poems for his prodigal conduct. He received many local honors, among them designation as a courtier to several native potentates, but the British regarded him with suspicion and snubbed him. He died at the age of seventy-one, and Saksena, remarking on certain hardships of his hero's life, observes, "No wonder that he sought solace in his moderate cups."

1971

V

*The Train Had Just Arrived
at Malgudi Station*

WHEN I WAS VISITING MY HOME, IN NEW
Delhi, a while back, I considered making a journey to
the state of Mysore, a thousand miles to the south, to see
R. K. Narayan, the writer, but my pilgrimage got lost
in my empty pockets. I wanted to meet Narayan not
because he had written eleven novels and produced two
volumes of short stories, not because he was acclaimed
the best novelist in India (fiction-writing is a fledgling
art in my country), not even because he had the reputation of being something of a saint (there are too many
poseurs in Hindustan), but for an almost obsessive personal reason. I was drawn to Narayan because his books,
though they were written in English, a language foreign
to most of his countrymen and also to most of his characters, had the ring of true India in them. He had succeeded where his peers had failed, and this without re-
lying on Anglicized Indians or British caricatures to
people his novels. My fascination with his art was personal, for, as I had written him, "like you, I find myself,
but only now and again, writing as an Indian for an
audience thousands of miles away, spectators with moods
and habits so different from our own that it is not easy to

be more than a tourist guide to them." For me, the magic of his unpretentious, almost unliterary novels was his astonishing marriage of opposite points of the compass. My wish to know him was fulfilled in New York, when I picked up my telephone one summer afternoon and heard a soft voice from the other end: "Um! This is Narayan. 'If the mountain will not come to Mohammed, Mohammed will go to the mountain.' You know, we are living practically next door to one another. I am just a couple of blocks away from you. Um! Can I come over?"

Within a few minutes, Narayan was at my apartment, on East Fifty-eighth Street. A neither too stout nor too lean figure, he strolled in rather boyishly. One shoulder appeared to be lower than the other, and his lilting walk recalled the end of the Bharat Natyam, an Indian classical dance in which the performer finishes by returning to the place where he took his first step, his shoulders gracefully preceding his legs in a swaying motion. Narayan dropped into my best armchair and, with a smile revealing a great many polished teeth, said, "I feel at home. Um! Do you?" I had to laugh.

Narayan, who was fifty-five, had a sharp face, with full lips, a slightly hooked nose, and a very impressive forehead, capped with thinning gray hair. The most noticeable thing about his face, however, was his eyes, impish and mischievous, peering out from behind thick, black-rimmed glasses. His body was loosely, carelessly clothed in nondescript gray trousers, a tweed jacket, and a white shirt, which was oddly finished off with an improvised tie pin, a piece of red thread wound around one shirt button. If it were not that he had the wheat-colored complexion of a Brahman, he might pass unnoticed in India as an anonymous member of the roving multitude; only a constant expression of innocence and a certain elusiveness about him saved him from seeming bland.

I asked him if he would like a cigarette. He flashed his teeth in a quick smile and said, "Once upon a time I used to smoke, and then one day it struck me how ridiculous it was for a grown-up man to have fire between his teeth—now puffing, now inhaling. Once this thought had lodged in my mind, I couldn't light a cigarette. It seemed so silly that I broke into a laugh at the thought of it, which was actually a tickle." He flashed his teeth again. "New York is the absolute yend in the summer," he said. "I should come here wonly in the winter. What is this—Consolidated Edison digging the ground, jets overhead, soot in the air, trucks running people down, no place to walk, and no children in the streets? It's hotter than the inside of an engine. I shall leave very soon. Oh, Lard, all one can do in this city is barricade oneself in an air-conditioned room. It is the absolute yend." As Narayan talked on, I discovered that he spoke a certain sort of Indian English; he made some of his "o"s into "a"s, and prefixed "y" and "w," respectively, to words beginning with "e" and "o." It gave his English a soft, balmy tone.

"You know, it's a beautiful season in my Mysore now," he continued. "The monsoon is just breaking, and the winter breeze is yeverywhere." Narayan went on to explain that Mysore, the capital of the onetime princely

state of Mysore, is about twenty-five hundred feet above
sea level. The Cauvery, one of the biggest rivers in India,
coils around the capital so that one cannot travel eight or
ten miles away from the city in any direction without
coming upon it. Mysore has probably not changed in at
least a thousand years, and the landscape of the place has
not yet been manicured by industrial implements; the
countryside encircles Mysore with a dense and snug
forest. The only inroad the twentieth century has made
in this town is in the installation of underground drain-
age, water tanks, and electric power. Mysore nestles at
the foot of a hill a thousand feet tall, which has a temple
on its crest. Both hill and temple are named after the
goddess Chamundi, the patron deity of the two hundred
and fifty thousand inhabitants of Mysore. Narayan then
told me that when the demon Mahisha, taking the form
of a buffalo, threatened the world with destruction—he
had the ability to produce demon buffaloes as numerous
as the drops of his blood—the goddess Chamundi came
charging on a lion with swords and lances. She managed
to kill the fiend, and her lion licked up all his blood
before it could multiply itself into countless likenesses of
him. A millennium ago, King Raya Chamundi, who took
the name of the savior, carved out a thousand steps in the
side of the hill for the convenience of her votaries. As a
youth, Narayan often ran up the steps, taking thirty or
forty minutes to reach the temple. "Comparatively recently, they also built a five- or six-mile road leading up
to the temple," Narayan said proudly. "The way is well
lighted, and at night the home of Chamundi gleams like a
lighthouse."

I asked Narayan whether he would like some tea.

"A little later," he said, taking out of his pocket a small Kodak film box. "I carry my lifeblood in this." He shook the box and then took out an areca, or betel nut, which he sucked happily, like a child relishing a sweet. "You know, I find that my pen moves only when I have a betel nut in my mouth," he said. "Without one, I can neither think nor write."

I asked him if he had always lived in Mysore.

"No, no, we are not Kannadiga, yindigenous to Mysore," he said. "We are Tamilians, from the province of Madras. And our family's ascent from a village to Madras, the capital city, took many generations. I have no sense of history, but I know that my initial 'R' stands for Rasipuram, the village which must have housed my ancestors." Neither he nor his characters are villagers, he said; rather, they are *hommes de ville*. Narayan has no illusions about noble rustics. As far as he is concerned, villagers' lives are monotonous and sedentary, and there is no story waiting in a village, the birthplace of a good novel being a halfway house between a static village and an anonymous industrial city. "By the time I came into the family, my kinsmen were happily urbanized," Narayan said. "In fact, soon after my arrival, my father, Krishnaswami Iyer—'K' in my name—followed many of his classfellows from Madras University to idyllic Mysore, where there were greater job opportunities. My mother, Gnanambal, who was very weak and was about to have another child, took my brothers and sisters to Mysore, but since I was very small she left me behind in Madras with my grandmother, whom I called

Ammani—that is, Madam. I soon established myself as her favorite, and was still living there long after my mother was well."

Narayan's first novel, "Swami and Friends," published in 1935, when he was twenty-nine, grew out of his urchin days at Ammani's. Until this book was written, his surname was Narayanswami, but the publishers, not wanting the novel to be confused with an autobiography, persuaded Narayanswami to drop the "swami" ("religious leader") from his name. The plain "Narayan" has always served as both his first and his last name, since, according to custom, he could not be called by the appellation of his father or of a village. He was the only child in the house, and Ammani, instead of disciplining him, gorged him with sweetmeats and, when he was especially good, with betel nuts. Kunjappa ("Little Fellow"), as she called him, grew up into a wild, idle lad who, in preference to studying his lessons in arithmetic and English grammar, swung like a monkey in a tree from one rafter of Ammani's tall, spreading house to another. "The house was built around an enormous Indian-style courtyard," Narayan told me. "Its doors were thick teakwood slabs four feet wide and six or seven feet high, covered with studs and ornaments, and flanking the doors were matching smooth pillars crowned with little brass figures of monkeys, elephants, eagles, and pigeons. I would climb up the columns, jump from door to door, raise myself to another tier by the balustrade, and wander from one empty room to another. Ammani could never find me." Kunjappa did put in fairly regular appearances at the Christian Mission

School, where he learned to love the Hindu gods simply because the chaplain extolled the Christian God and made fun of what Narayan called "His Indian brothers and sisters." The chaplain ridiculed Ganesa for having an elephant's head, Hanuman for having a monkey's body, and Krishna for habitually stealing butter and chasing girls. "What sort of gods are these?" the chaplain would say. And when Kunjappa once boldly asked the chaplain "Why was Christ crucified if He was so much better?" the missionary slapped the blasphemous boy and sent him spinning out of the room. "I was thinking the other day why it is that I can't write a novel without Krishna, Ganesa, Hanuman, astrologers, pundits, temples, and devadasis, or temple prostitutes," Narayan said. "Do you suppose I have been trying to settle my score with the old boy? Um! In any case, that has turned out to be my India."

Kunjappa's father, who was the headmaster of the government school in Mysore, finally got news of the boy's idleness, and sent for him. He took his son by the ear and gave him a tour of his own extensive library. Kunjappa was not impressed. At his new school and then at Mysore University, Narayanswami sat daydreaming, looking out of the window at trees and passersby, listening to nothing, reading practically nothing; the only book that made an impression on his vegetating mind was Rabindranath Tagore's romantic tract against academic education. He failed his intermediate and baccalaureate examinations several times, finally managing to receive his Bachelor of Arts degree at twenty-four—a shameful age for an Indian. His elder brother Srinivas had received his at eighteen, and many Madrasi boys were Bachelors of Arts at fifteen or sixteen. (Narayan's long college career provided material for his second novel, "Bachelor of Arts," whose publication, in 1937, marked the beginning of his reputation as an author in England.)

I asked Narayan again whether he would like some tea.

"If it isn't too much bother," he said.

I invited him to walk with me to a nearby shop for some pastry.

He was disappointed that we were not going to do our errand by subway. "You know," he said, wiping his forehead with his sleeve, "I like travelling underground, because the people there remind me of the crowds in our bazaars. Except that the subterranean travellers are much more intense and purposeful—they are always going to some definite job in a rush."

In the pastry shop, Narayan quickly made friends with the saleslady, who was Swedish, and he accepted an impulsive invitation she extended to him for dinner the following week. Aside to me, he said, "Yevery day I like to meet a new person." His innocent face lighted up at the sight of pineapple pastry, and he carried it back to the apartment himself.

When I had put some water on to boil, he asked me if I had read his story "A Breach of Promise," and I told him I had. "That was almost my first tale," he said. "It is very truthful—autobiographical, you know. It concerns a student, myself, who fails a lot of examinations." The story is set in Chamundi Temple. There is an Indian superstition that a perfect work of art invites the wrath of the gods. To placate the deities, the ancient Indian sculptors chopped off a toe or a finger of a statue. Similarly, the beauty of the perfect temple is carefully marred by two monstrous gargoyles that squat on its tower. They have enormous rolling tongues, flashing eyes, and ugly noses. The hero of "A Breach of Promise," resolving to take his life, scales the hill and then the temple tower, and straddles a gargoyle's tongue, which is as large as a platform. "In reaching the tongue of death, he has somehow skinned his elbow, and just when he has poised himself for the big jump, the sight of blood on his arm frightens the boy, and he shuffles back into the room of the tower," Narayan explained. "I like to conclude my stories with such things when I can. I don't remember if, after one of my exam failures, I got as far as the gargoyle's tongue, but I do remember scribbling my name in charcoal on the wall of the tower room, for posterity. I never had any intention of committing suicide, so the whole thing was farcical. That's the way life is in our temples and our houses."

The water reached its boiling point in a snoring whistle, and Narayan jumped. When I explained the simple mechanism of the kettle, he said, "Oh, Lard, what is this modernity, all these gadgets and such?"

I poured him out some tea and sliced the pastry for him. He drank the tea in long, noisy sips and ate with two fingers. He has small, feminine hands, and as he lifted his cup, his little finger flew out. (His hand looked more natural than its genteel counterparts in Kensington spinsterdom.) He wore two rings on the last two fingers of his left hand; one had a sapphire inset, and the other was a plain gold band. I asked him about them.

"This sapphire one is an heirloom, a hundred years old," he said. "I received it on my wedding day. My father-in-law, Nagswara Iyer, who, incidentally, was also a headmaster, gave it to me, and he got it from his father-in-law. The gold band I received from my wife at her deathbed. Her name was Rajam." As he spoke her name, tears came into his eyes.

I poured him another cup of tea, and for some minutes he remained silent.

It seemed to me after a while that he wanted to talk about his wife. "How did you meet her, Narayan?" I asked.

He cleared his throat, took a bite of pastry, munched it, and said, smiling his prompt smile, "I escarted my elder sister Janaki from Mysore to nearby Coimbatore, where her husband was a practicing advocate. While I was standing at the carner of the equivalent of a big-city mall there, I saw a girl about eighteen. She was tall and slim and had classical features; her face had the finish and perfection of sculpture. She walked past me as in a dance. I kept looking for a gargoyle or some such imperfection, but there was none. It was spring and I was twenty-eight. I suppose that had something to do with my falling completely and instantly in love with her. But when I myself, instead of my parents, approached her mother and father, they were outraged at my picking my own wife, the unconventionality of my love. But they asked me what was going to be my profession, what means I had for supporting a wife. I said simply, 'I write.' In those days, no one could own up to writing stories in India. It was the most penniless thing one could do. After some pressure from my family, Rajam's parents did consult their astrologer, who immediately declared that my horoscope showed that I would be either a polygamist or a widower. I forced the issue. I found another astrologer, who went into ecstasies at the sight of rupees. He was an accomplished debater and defeated the other pundit, and Rajam's parents, realizing that I was from a good and large family, and that, whatever happened to me, she would always be taken care of, gave in to the marriage."

Rajam and Narayan were a happy couple. Like a good Indian wife, she did not show public affection for Narayanswami, and her attention was distributed equally among his mother, his father, and his three younger brothers—Balram, Ramachandar, and Laxman —who were still at college. (Laxman is now one of the better-known cartoonists in India.) He also had two sisters, Janaki and Alamelu, and two older brothers, Srinivas and Pattabhi, but the sisters had married and were settled in homes of their own, and the older brothers had moved away (one to take a job in a fertilizer plant, the other to take a government position), so Rajam was spared the need to spread her affection further. Narayanswami spent most of his time sitting and talking with his family, and after the birth of his daughter, Hema, he spent hours every day watching her in her cot or on her mat. Now and again, he stole a couple of hours to do a little writing in an upstairs room, but even then he called out for his wife every half hour or so to bring him Hema and some coffee. Rajam could not read English, the only language in which Narayan found he could write. Nevertheless, she took a keen interest in his hundreds of rejection slips and, later, in the reviews of his books—"Swami and Friends," "Bachelor of Arts," and, in 1939, his third novel, "The Dark Room," which dealt with a Hindu wife who submits passively to a positive or inconsiderate (depending on which side of the Suez one lives on) husband.

"But the prophecy of her family astrologer turned out to be right," Narayan said sadly. "My father-in-law, who was quite well-to-do, wanted to settle a house on Rajam, and one day he came up from Coimbatore and we went around searching for a place. We looked through a number of remodelled houses, and late that afternoon we happened upon one that seemed suitable. It had the solidity of an wold house and the bright cleanness of a new one. While my father-in-law and I were canvassing the land, Rajam went into the bathroom, an outhouse, to wash. She did not rejoin us. I got worried and walked back to the bathroom. Rajam was pounding away at the shut door, screaming, 'Someone open it! Someone open it!' I gave the door one or two hard kicks and Rajam fell out in my arms. She was convulsed with sobs, and her face was a feverish red. She cried out that it was the dirtiest place she had ever been in. She said a fly had settled on her lips. I took her home, but she wouldn't yeat anything. She kept washing herself, time and time again. By the evening, she had a temperature, and she remained in bed with typhoid for twenty days. It was 1939, and no one had heard of chloramphenicol.

Rajam died. A fly had killed an almost five-year-old marriage."

Narayan said that he considered following her onto the funeral pyre, but there was Hema, the very likeness of Rajam. For the next few years, Narayan battled with the fact of death. He periodically left Mysore for Madras, where he met a lawyer who claimed to communicate with the dead through so-called automatic writing. The lawyer transcribed messages from Rajam.

"He was no hoax," Narayan said. "For one thing, he wrote three or four thousand words in a half hour, and no man can compose so much so quickly. For another, Rajam, through the automatic writing, gave proofs of her yexistence by such precise instructions as 'Give the brooch lying in the tortoise-shell box on the third shelf of my mother's cupboard to such-and-such a beggar woman.' When she entered the room to dictate, the air current changed perceptibly. I could breathe her presence. Since that time, I have lost all distinction between life and death."

After a moment's silence, he continued, "But the therapy did not really yend until I published my fourth novel, 'The English Teacher,' in 1945. It was all about my life with Rajam." The concluding chapters of the book were concerned with the psychic experiments, and the English critics lashed out at them. "Of course," Narayan said, "the reviewers did not realize that the whole story was autobiographical—that I myself had been a witness to the experiments. But what's the use?" He sighed. "You don't believe it, yeither."

I asked Narayan to stay for dinner. He said, "Thank

you very much. Thank you very much. But no. I'm a vegetarian and am completely South Indian in my eating habits. When I eat out in this country, I mostly go hungry." He said he would dine with me some other day, when I had mastered his dietary ways.

I walked Narayan home. We strolled half a block out of our way to wave goodbye to the saleslady in the pastry shop. "Isn't it lucky that I eat yeggs?" he said, smiling with his eyes and teeth. "Wotherwise, I would never have gone there and made friends with the Swedish lady." At the corner of Third Avenue and Fifty-eighth Street, a new building was going up. Narayan took one look at the Consolidated Edison workers who were digging up the street, and put both his hands up to his ears. He didn't take them down until we had turned east on Fifty-seventh Street. "Oh, Lard, this is equally noisy," he said, glaring at the two-way traffic.

To take his mind off the noise and America, I said, "Narayan, why is it that your books don't show a trace of Western influence?" I told him I had also been struck by the fact that he hardly ever touched on politics, of either British or free India. Except for a Mr. Brown and an American journalist in "The Guide," published in 1958, I could recall no foreigners in his books, I said, and his Indians had the logic and idiom, and the ambitions, not of the scientific West but of the almost agrarian East.

"To be a good writer anywhere, you must have roots—both in religion and in family," Narayan replied thoughtfully. "I have these things. I am rooted to the right triangle of Madras, Mysore, and Coimbatore, none of them much more than a couple of hundred miles distant from the others." For the first forty-nine years of his life, he had stayed within the boundaries of the triangle, he said as, taking advantage of a green light, we dashed across Second Avenue, and he had passed most of his life in the communism of the joint-family life, where everything was owned in common and no one asked questions about income.

"But must one have such ties?" I asked. "What about the expatriate Steins and Hemingways, and all those Irish writers who have worked successfully away from their homeland?"

"I have not read many of them, but I am sure they have nothing to say to me," Narayan said emphatically. They could have had no religion, no values, no feelings, he went on. His greatest test of a good author was his "readability." Tolstoy, Joyce, and Faulkner were all "bores." He had read a hundred pages of "War and Peace" and could not understand why E. M. Forster considered Tolstoy a happy god who could play with the entire world. Shakespeare was readable and fun only in paperbacks, where there were no footnotes and things like that. There were no Indian novelists to speak of. Indian writers were either too "Westernized" or too "deliberate." "I can't like any writing that's deliberate. If an author is deliberate, then I can't read him—he's not readable," Narayan concluded.

We paused at the Fifty-seventh Street approach to the Queensboro Bridge. There was an unbroken stream of rush-hour cars. "This is the worst intersection in New

York," Narayan said. "Why can't they put more policemen here? This crossing paralyzes me. My two favorite
avenues are on the West Side, around Twenty-third
Street. I like the Ninth Avenue, which is like Madras,
and the Tenth, because it reminds me of Bombay. Why
do you suppose that is?"

I said I didn't know, since there could be no architec-
tural resemblance; perhaps it was because of the children
and the slums. "But then you should like Hemingway," I
said, picking up our conversation about good writers.
"Isn't he immensely readable?"

Narayan broke into a wheezing laugh. "You must
allow me my contradictions. I contradict myself all the
time."

"Do you find Hemingway deliberate?"

"From the little I have read, I shouldn't think so." We
waded across the bridge approach. "I don't read much,
because I don't want to be influenced. I suppose my
wonly love is Graham Greene. I've read most of his
things, because he's my champion and my best English
friend." I knew that it was thanks to Greene's support
that Narayan was first published. "Novels may bore me,
but never people. To me, all individuals are like characters in my own stories, with whom one has to live for
many pages of writing, even if they stop being interesting after a while."

We reached the apartment house that Narayan was
living in, on East Fifty-seventh Street. He invited me
into his vestibule, which was a little larger than a telephone booth. "You may have gathered that I'm not an
academic sort," he said, his words rebounding from the

walls. "In fact, I don't like graduate students writing theses on me. They always try to read meaning into my books, trace a theme, relate this character to that, make a connection between hero and hero. I wish they would leave me and my books alone. And now I must go and prepare my dinner upstairs, which for me here is not a family ritual but a lonely meal." Breaking into his smile (very much like Rosie, the heroine of "The Guide," whose smile he had called an "open sesame" to her future), he added, "For twenty-seven years, except for short periods when I was away, I ate three meals a day from the same silver platter, which I'd received at my marriage. The platter was too heavy to carry across to America." He said it would embarrass him to have company while he cooked and ate his vegetarian meal, so I made arrangements to visit him the next evening.

As I walked back to my flat after three or four hours with Narayan, I couldn't help marvelling at him. He seemed to carry his home, his cosmos, on his back, as did the ageless swamis.

I dropped in on Narayan after dinner on the following day. He was so inept with mechanical devices that he kept his finger firmly on the buzzer unlocking the front door until he saw me step out of the lift on his floor.

"Woh, you've arrived," he said, his eyes twinkling. He showed me into his one-room apartment, which he was borrowing from Harvey Breit, the former assistant editor of the New York *Times Book Review*, who used it for a retreat from a larger apartment, on Park Avenue. For America, the room seemed bare; there was a painting by William Walton (given to Breit by Hemingway), a framed article of Breit's ("The Haunting Drama of Dylan Thomas") from the magazine section of the New York *Times*, and a small collection of books. The floor was covered with a neutral bluish-green carpet, and for furniture there were a couple of canvas chairs, a studio couch, and a small table, which was loaded like a mule with the results of Narayan's day's shopping—Uncle Ben's rice, Aunt Jemima's pancake mix, a variety of Indian herbs and spices, and jars of pickled onions and mangoes. Narayan rapturously explained that during his morning walk he had found a most splendid international food shop at Twenty-eighth Street and Third Avenue. "They carry all the Indian things except quality betel nuts," he said. "I made some good friends there, with Indians who come there regularly for supplies. Incidentally, once I meet a person I always like to keep in touch. I've spent most of my days in my room telephoning all my friends and acquaintances in this city. I write everyone's name and telephone number in my diary as soon as I get to know him. I have all sorts of friends. There are the Breits, who give me hospitality in America, and Santha and Faubion Bowers, who love me for myself, and Donald Keene, professor of Japanese at Columbia, who visited me in Mysore." There were John and Jane Gunther, who, he said, liked his novels; Greta Garbo, who took him to be a specimen of the mystic East; Cal Whipple, editor of *Life's* International Edition, who thought him a good reporter on India; Marshall Best, the editorial vice-president of the Viking Press, who was interested in him as an author on his list; Helen

Strauss, the literary agent with the William Morris Agency, who regarded him as a valuable client; Allene Talmey, of *Vogue*, who "memorized" his books; Lyle Blair, of the Michigan State University Press, who first published him in America and didn't want Narayan to be "commercialized." Then, he had scores and scores of acquaintances (most of whom had not read his books) in the New York Indian colony, including people in government service, in commerce, and in the universities. "Like true reality, I am many things to many men," he said. "Shall we sit down?"

I leaned back in one of the canvas chairs; he perched on the other. Narayan was barefoot. He proudly held up his pair of shoes for my inspection. "I got these at Saxone, in England, five years ago. The shoes have been resoled only once." He put the worn shoes down affectionately and offered me a betel nut. I took one and began to chew it, whereupon he admonished me to suck it slowly. Narayan was dressed in an ill-fitting brown suit he had picked up that morning for forty-three dollars at a clothing store on lower Seventh Avenue.

"I have written the first page of my new novel today, while waiting in the shop for my suit to be altered," he said. The story had begun to form in his head when one of his friends, a lawyer, was handling a lawsuit that a wasteful son had brought against his indulgent father, a prosperous sweetmeat dealer, to get more money from him. In the new novel, Narayan's merchant was to be similarly taxed in both pocket and endurance by his debauched son, until he decided to abandon his boy and do penance for the sins of his ancestors and progeny by building a temple. But in the path of godly service, too, he was to run into difficulties. He would be swindled by corrupt contractors and prehensile bricklayers. "Such are the ways of the world and of my novels," Narayan said, chuckling. "You might say my sweetmeat dealer is defeated in his purpose by the scratch of silver rupees on the elbows of anyone and yeveryone. The actual sweetmeat dealer may build a temple yet." Narayan laughed. The strange thing was, he said, that actual people, without ever setting eyes on his books, did fall in line with their plots. There was the remarkable instance of Margayya, the central character of "The Financial Expert," published in 1952. In the first pages of the book, he was almost the exact double of a real Margayya. Narayan had observed this kindly financial wizard at work in the shade of a banyan tree, which he used as an office in lending small sums of money to various illiterate peasants, who squatted in a semicircle around him. They preferred his personal, if antiquated, style of lending money—always for a small fee—to the cold formalism of the Central Coöperative Land Mortgage Bank, around the corner. Margayya becomes a fictional character when the bank officials, feeling their jobs and system threatened by his methods, try to drive him out of business, and when his son, Balu, in a tantrum, throws his father's only account book into a drain. A deity answers Margayya's prayers for assistance by making him the publisher and salesman of a pornographic book, "Bed Life, or, The Science of Marital Happiness"—or, as Margayya euphemistically retitles it for publication, "Domestic Harmony." "The choice of a smutty profession for Margayya was an extraordinary premonition on my part," Narayan now told me gleefully. "I saw him recently. He was hawking books of popular film tunes, which are the only best-sellers we have in India. Hidden under the leaflets were two-anna obscene books." And this, Narayan said, was by no means the only time that life had imitated his art.

I asked Narayan if he was ever oppressed by a sense of diminishing literary powers or powers of prophecy.

"Woh, no," he said. "I really have more stories than I can write in a lifetime, and probably in the next *janma*"— incarnation—"I will be not an author but a publisher." He smiled, and then suddenly stood up. "It's too noisy here!" he exclaimed. He shut the window, but the room faced Fifty-seventh Street and nothing could seal out the roar of the traffic. He returned to his canvas seat, discouraged. "How nice it would be to live in Malgudi," he said.

Malgudi is the domain of Narayan's imagination. There is no such town in any directory, almanac, or atlas of the subcontinent. There is a Lalgudi in Madras province, but Narayan says that the similarity of the two names is a coincidence. As the setting of his dozen books, Malgudi corresponds to Faulkner's Yoknapatawpha County. The resemblance, however, is remote, because Malgudi is an infinitely simple place, and because its landmarks—the Albert Mission College, the Regal Haircutting Saloon, the railway station, the temple, the bazaars, the lead statue of Sir Frederick Lawley, the Central Coöperative Land Mortgage Bank, the office of the *Banner* (a newspaper), the huts of the Harijans (children of God) in which Gandhi stayed, Market Road, Kabir Lane, the Taj Hotel, the banyan-tree office, the river steps, Mempi Hill—all, from book to book, chaotically change position. Compared to Faulkner's spiritual home, Malgudi is quiet, dusty, and uneventful, lacking political and social problems, sexual outrages, and hundreds of other things. The dominant force in Malgudi is ineluctable fate, playing one ironic trick after another on the simple inhabitants, who rise and fall, a little blandly, as fortune dictates. But the bland cosmos of Malgudi is blessed with grace, because its people are innocent and comic—copies of Narayan, with his dazzling smile fixed on their faces.

"You know," Narayan told me, "I remember waking up with the name Malgudi on Vijayadasami, the day on which the initiation of learning is celebrated." It was in September, 1930, he said, that the name of the town had been vouchsafed him by the divine patrons of knowledge. "Malgudi was an yearth-shaking discovery for me, because I had no mind for facts and things like that, which would be necessary in writing about Lalgudi or any real place. I first pictured not my town but just the railway station, which was a small platform with a banyan tree, a stationmaster, and two trains a day, one coming and one going. On Vijayadasami, I sat down and wrote the first sentence about my town: 'The train had just arrived at Malgudi station.' But it was some years before I could write the opening words of 'Swami and Friends': 'It was Monday morning.' The sentence about the train got revised." Since that Vijayadasami, the town boundaries had expanded to take in streets, people, industries. "Many academicians are hard at work trying to find where, exactly, Malgudi might be situated," Narayan said, all his teeth shining in a smile. "My books are full of contradictory leads. Once, a researcher wrote to ask me how long it took to go from Malgudi to Madras by train. I wrote back that the train journey from Mysore to Madras was fourteen hours but that it took Margayya more than twice as long to get from Malgudi to Madras. I never heard from that gentleman again."

I said I thought one could cover the entire perimeter of his right triangle in a couple of days.

He smiled happily, and offered me a betel nut. "Don't feel guilty at sharing this elixir with me," he said, and he went on to explain that he had taken precautions against running short of betel nuts on this visit to America, which was his third. After his first visit, when he was without them for six months, he had made arrangements with his mother to buy some from his favorite shop in Mysore and send them to him by air. His main problem was to convince the American customs officers that he was not getting a consignment of dope.

I put one in my mouth and sucked it, as he had instructed me to do. He was very much pleased, and offered me coffee, which I accepted.

"I think of myself as the globe's best coffee taster," Narayan explained through the kitchen door. "I can't tell wine from beer; all alcohol seems poison to me. But I know the vineyards of coffee beans in southern India well. I can distinguish them by a sip." He turned on a tap. "You know," he continued, "I read somewhere the other day that the cause of cancer is frozen meat. Is it true?"

"Some causes of cancer, at least, come and go," I said. "There is a flurry of controversy about lipsticks one month, waxed milk containers the next, and—"

"Oh, really? Still, it comforts me to be a vegetarian." After fumbling with a box of matches for some time, he finally had the stove lighted. But he remained in the kitchen to watch the kettle. "You know, I wish I had an apartment like this in Mysore—clean, neat, and compact," he said. "As it is, I have an enormous house, which I built six or seven years ago." He told me that his house, which was on the edge of the city and was surrounded by wilderness, occupied half of a three-quarter-acre plot. He was thinking of building a replica of Breit's one-room apartment on the other half and moving into it, for the house, which had five bedrooms, four bathrooms, a big drawing room and dining room, and servants' quarters—modern ones—in the basement, remained empty for half the year, when he was travelling or was visiting his daughter, Hema, now married and living in Coimbatore. He could not understand why, but ever since he made his first journey to America (in response to repeated invitations from Chadbourne Gilpatric, of the Rockefeller Foundation), in 1955, and gave Hema in marriage a year later, he had been restless.

The water boiled, and, after much clattering and shuffling, Narayan brought two coffee cups to the table. He held his cup in a gingerly manner and drank the coffee slowly. "I originally built my house in the hope of getting all my family to move there," he said. "But my mother wouldn't hear of it, because she was frightened of the woods around me and also did not really like the thought of giving up her old way of living." So, Narayan went on, he had never taken the trouble to furnish the place. He had just carried in a few chairs, a table, and a bed, and given one of the rooms a semblance of life. He spent as little time in the room as possible, because he missed his family, even though he visited them daily. (They lived only fifteen minutes away.) He used his one habitable room as a sort of retreat for writing. "It's quite nice," he said. "I can see the countryside around me for more than ten miles."

Narayan told me about his Mysore day. It begins with a three- or four-hour stroll. He considers his morning walk his office hours, because he stops and talks to people, many of whom chat with him freely about their doings or their troubles, or give him advice about renting his house (empty houses bring bad luck) or about making profits on his books, which they cannot read. Only a few ask him for practical help, probably because they know him to be a mere writer; most demand his ear and his sympathy. If, on his promenade, Narayan sees three or four men in a huddle, he observes their ways closely. In his many years of living in Mysore, he has made friends among artisans, businessmen, lawyers, teachers—the men and women of his novels. After lunch, he may do an hour or two of writing—his limit for a day's serious work. He composes fast, and two thousand words in a couple of hours is not an unusual achievement for him. "I am an inattentive, quick writer who has little sense of style," he said candidly. Once he has written the first few pages of a novel, he seldom retouches a sentence, believing that writing is "a dovetailing process," by which he means that a novel well begun writes itself. After his writing, he meditates, and his barren room is especially suited to that. He begins his exercises by reading a little bit of the *puranas*, or Sanskrit sacred poems, after which he repeatedly recites to himself the Gayatri Mantra, a prayer to the light that illuminates the sun to illuminate all minds. After he has had a short rest, the late afternoon finds him at his family's house; he dines, then makes the rounds of his intimate friends, and goes home to bed.

"I've been talking to you like Railway Raju," Narayan said, referring to the tourist-guide saint who is the hero of "The Guide." "I sometimes feel like him; it is difficult not to, especially when I'm telling about Mysore, which I know better than any other place." As he finished his coffee, he added that some family incidents and his own character had given him the conception of Raju (successively a tramp; a guide to the historical sights of Malgudi; the savior, seducer, and manager of Rosie; an unfortunate jailbird; and an unwilling rainmaker and saint), and that Rosie (a wavering Hindu wife and a great classical dancer) and her husband, Marco (who prefers ancient pictures of dancers to the beauty and genius of his wife), had a similar genesis.

It was very late, and over Fifty-seventh Street hung a sort of Malgudi hush, shattered only now and again by the clap of a passing truck. Narayan yawned a little, and we stood up. "Have some more betel nuts," he said as he fitted one of them into each side of his mouth. He tilted his film box over my hand and shook out two more, like a man throwing dice who is confident that luck will not let him down. "Someone was telling me the other day that in this country all good writers have to be unhappy to write well," he said. "Why is that? I find I write best when I have no burden on my mind, when I am absolutely at peace with myself. That's why for many years after Rajam died I couldn't write anything."

At the door, we embraced each other in the Indian way, and he started ringing the door buzzer again to call the lift up. I took him into the hallway and showed him the right button. "All this gadgetry confounds me," he said as the automatic door closed.

A couple of days later, Narayan dropped in on me. First, we sucked a couple of betel nuts together, and then we dined; an Indian friend had cooked a vegetarian meal for us and left it in the oven. Narayan ate his rice, vegetable curry, and yoghurt in silence; from time to time he rested his fork on the plate, as though he were about to tell me something, only to resume eating. He seemed depressed. After we had finished dinner, he said slowly, "I'm troubled about the dramatization of 'The Guide,' but I really don't know where to begin."

Not wanting to press him, I merely served him some coffee, which he did not drink.

"Oh, Lard," he said after a while. "I feel a little bit like Raju, whose wonderful career and affair with Rosie, in 'The Guide,' came to an yend because of a small forgery, a little technicality. How nature imitates art!"

He smiled. "I sometimes find myself preferring the Indian literary life to the American."

"What does the Indian literary life have to do with Raju?" I asked.

"Nothing, nothing," Narayan said. "There is no such thing as the Indian literary life." He smiled again, dazzlingly. There were vernacular writers and poets, he explained, but there was no methodical criticism in the provincial languages, since the Indians were not as rigorous as English and American critics in separating the wheat from the chaff when it came to Indian writers working in English. This meant that the men of letters writing in underdeveloped languages had neither fame nor audience and probably no critical tradition (in the Western sense), and so, possibly, had no compulsion to improve themselves—or, indeed, to write at all. As for Indian literature in English—which had never been more than a trickle—it was on its way out with the raj language itself. Narayan said that for him the only thrill that the Indian literary life—if it could be called that— had to offer was an occasional letter from a magazine editor whom he had never met that went something like this: "My dear Narayan, I have taken a great deal of pride and interest in your long and astounding career and feel a personal investment in all your manifold and multifarious achievements, which bring a great deal of credit to our great country, and, indeed, to me personally, since I've always thought of you as part of my family. We are going to press with a special children's supplement. Undoubtedly you would not wish to be absent from its table of contents, and undoubtedly we would not wish you to be. Of course, we will not be able to pay you as much as your greatly deserving genius warrants, but we hope the postal order of fifty rupees that will follow the receipt of your submission will be taken as a token of our abiding faith and pride in your works and person. With warmest regards. Yours affectionately . . .'' "And then," Narayan said, "years after the 'submission'—never acknowledged—when no postal arder has reached me, if I drop a line to the editor about the promised sum, he will immediately spread the word that 'Narayan is mercenary.' What a strange and wonderful country we come from!"

I remarked that Narayan was to the Indian literary landscape what Daniel Defoe was to the English, and then asked how a writer survived in that strange and wonderful country.

The answer was that he did not, unless he had a private income, an indulgent family, or some sort of job. Narayan's father, a learned headmaster, whose heroes were Thomas Carlyle and Walter Pater, tried to force his son into earning a living by pushing him first in one direction and then in another, but Narayan's first experience as a teacher soured him on that profession for life. He was paralyzed with fear at the sight of the burly boys, was tongue-tied during lessons, and was insolent to his permissive headmaster, who merely asked him to stay with the class, even when he had nothing to say, for a full period, rather than dismiss it after a few minutes. Narayan also balked at joining the civil service, because he was sure he hadn't the patience, the presence, or the discipline—the triple *sine qua non* of officialdom. An attempt he made to become a sub-editor was foiled because, as it happened, the chief requirement for the position, in India, was a mastery of shorthand. Finally, Narayan resolved to "sell" himself no more, to do nothing—simply to write novels that neither Carlyle nor Pater nor his father would have been caught reading, and live off the joint-family system. Happily, his father loved him very much and was glad to have the do-nothing son at home. He died, however, without reading the manuscript of "Swami and Friends," which Narayan had never had the courage to show him. "But I remember that my father was very pleased at the sight of my book cover, which arrived just before his death," Narayan told me. "He also smiled whenever I showed him a small check or postal arder for a short story or an article." Narayan used to write tales for the *Hindu*, and occasionally did small news stories on sanitation, the law courts, scandals, and so on for *Justice*, a now defunct anti-Brahman newspaper. "Mr. Sampath" (a novel that appeared in the United States as "The Printer of Malgudi"), which he wrote and published in 1949, was a success, and he adapted it for a popular Indian film called "Mr. Sampath," with the actor Motilal and the actress Padmini. "I never sold myself into a job," Narayan said, "but people were buying me yeverywhere." Narayan got so tired of dealing with profiteers who passed as Indian publishers that at one point he started printing his own books. When he left me that evening, he was happily sucking betel nuts.

The next day, Narayan and I had both been asked to dinner by the Indian writer Santha Rama Rau, who is married to the American writer Faubion Bowers. When I arrived at the Bowers apartment, a walkup on East Ninety-fifth Street, I found Narayan there already. He was standing—looking like a little boy—between a low canvas chair and the tall Miss Rama Rau. She has an Indian complexion but was in European dress—stockings and a cotton frock. "Darling, how lovely to see you!" Miss Rama Rau said, taking my hand. "Isn't it jolly for three Indian writers to be able to have dinner together? I'm glad we were able to fit it in. I'm leaving for Hollywood in a day or two. Faubion and my son, Jai, have already started. Let's all sit down. You, darling," she said warmly, nodding at me, "come and sit beside me." Narayan perched on the canvas chair. Miss Rama Rau and I settled on a divan.

Miss Rama Rau asked Narayan what he had been doing lately, and he said he had met a demonstrative Indian donkey in the Central Park Zoo during his walk that morning. Narayan went on to tell us that the animal was just an ordinary *dhobi's* donkey, who, with his brethren, roamed the Indian streets by the million. But in America, apparently, he was a great success; nobody who saw him could doubt that the zoo-goers fed his vanity—an attribute never associated with donkeys in India. The donkey, however, had paid a price for his American importance; he had to live behind bars day and night. In Narayan's opinion, he was not happy. His incarceration frustrated him, and all day long, whenever he was not braying for his admiring audience, he flipped the lock of his cage with his tongue. In India, donkeys had an equally hard row to hoe. They were not treated mercifully. After carrying a big load all day, they were not fed but were put to pasture on the streets, where they ate not grass but discarded newspapers. So the choice for a donkey was poverty, a long day's work, and unhappiness in India or riches, self-expression, and unhappiness in America. If he were a horse, a camel, or an elephant, his alternatives would not be so limited. But in the reincarnation cycle prizes are more often reserved for those who fulfill their nature than for those who overreach themselves; a donkey is rewarded with a higher rebirth for being a mere donkey, not for competing with a peacock. "I think I'll write a little fable about him for *Harper's*," Narayan said, smiling. "Do you think they will take it?"

We smiled back, and then I asked Miss Rama Rau if she was going on a Hollywood holiday.

"No, no," she said. "I'm going there to write the next treatment of that mad Indian picture of mine. When I was in Madras with Narayan the last time, I received this exciting telegram from David O. Selznick to write the Jesus Christ-Mary Magdalene story for his wife, Jennifer Jones, to be set in India. Why India? You may well ask. One of those Hollywood coincidences, you know. Miss Jones—he always calls her Miss Jones—goes to India and loses her heart to it; meanwhile, David is approached to do the Christ-Magdalene picture, but refuses, because there are too many Christian films already. Then he has one of those fantastic, spooky inspirations: Why not shoot Christ and Magdalene in India, put the Christian story in a Hindu setting? And bingo! The idea takes wing and catches me in Madras. I read the telegram again and again, and wire back something to the effect that a religious picture in India is a giddy, jolly idea. Mad, but exciting stuff, don't you think?"

Narayan nodded benignly. I must have looked a little skeptical.

"Yes, darling," she said, fixing me with her gaze. "I thought the same. But, after all, wasn't Gandhi like Christ? Who else in two thousand years has caught the spirit of the Saviour so well? My story line is based on a disciple of the old boy's—naturally, a celibate. He thinks he knows everything about life until a lowdown American girl—in the film, Miss Jones—comes along, seduces him, and begins his education from scratch. I haven't worked out the details of this yet. But I think the whole thing is giddy. The idea is historical, universal. Here is the Saviour, Christ; here is Mahatma Gandhi; and here is the woman who ate the apple. I can be as pompous as the next woman."

Miss Rama Rau chatted on rapidly about the check that popped out of the mailbox every week, about the fairy-tale château on Sunset Boulevard awaiting her arrival in Hollywood, and about pending visits there of Garbo and the Gunthers. "Narayan, why don't you join the Hollywood party?" she asked.

Narayan said nothing.

"How about your usual tonic water, Narayan?" she went on. "There is no lime in the house. Will a little lemon do just as well?"

"That will be quite nice," Narayan said.

She turned to me, and I said I would take a little whiskey-and-soda.

Miss Rama Rau went into the kitchen. She returned and handed us our drinks. "Here, my darlings. Indians are inveterate talkers. We can't stop talking, talking, talking—a mile a minute. One of the reasons I left my Sixty-third Street apartment was that there was a dog who barked all day. His mistress used to wash him every few minutes and give him birthday parties, with paper napkins that had 'Happy Birthday, Doggie' written on them. She'd invite her neighbors to the parties. She used to call me Mrs. Bow-wow-wowers. I don't like animals. That's one sense in which I'm not Indian. Come on, foremost novelist, tell us a little bit about *you*."

Narayan laughed, flashing all his teeth. "You know," he said tentatively, "part of me is always somewhere else—in the paragraph I may write tomorrow, the character who has to be dovetailed into my novel—and then I am forever focussing my eyes on those vague, floating ideas that keep on buzzing in my head."

"Come on, foremost novelist," Miss Rama Rau said, "tell us the happiest and the saddest moment in your life. I asked my eight-year-old boy the same question the other day, and I was so touched to hear him say, in his American accent, that the happiest time was when I took him, for a short while, to India, and that the saddest was when he left India and my sister."

There was a silence, and then Narayan said matter-of-factly, "I suppose the saddest moment in my life was the passing of my wife."

We ate a simple vegetarian meal. After dinner, Narayan washed his hands and then strolled into the bedroom-nursery, where he squatted and played with

Miss Rama Rau's son's turtle. Narayan said that the philosophy of vegetarianism was based on a reverence for life—from turtles to human beings. "But I can qualify that a little," he added, smiling. "A reverence for a certain sort of moving life. You might say we are not supposed to yeat anything that moves horizontally. Happily, plants move vertically, skyward, and eggs drop from the chicken like rain from heaven." When we said good night to Miss Rama Rau, it was getting late, but she was still effervescent.

Downstairs, a taxi stopped for us, and we whizzed down Lexington Avenue to Fifty-seventh Street, where I went up with Narayan to his apartment for a quick after-dinner betel nut. When we were settled in our canvas chairs, I asked him to tell me about the dramatization of "The Guide," by Harvey Breit and his wife, Patricia Rinehart.

"It is a good play of its kind, but I now wish I weren't connected with it," he said. "I worry about it so much that I go to sleep at one and wake up at one-forty-five." Narayan rubbed his eyes like a child heavy with sleep. "Actually, there is one thing I haven't told you," he continued. "You see, I probably prefer 'The Guide' to be a quiet, serious production, with an Indian cast; in any case, I never cared about big names, and all that, but when Harvey told me about the money I could make on Broadway, I rather rashly promised my daughter and son-in-law and Minni—my little granddaughter—a trip to America if my play was successful."

At that moment, Narayan did look like a grandfather— benign and benevolent and slightly resigned—but whenever he smiled, he was again like a little boy from a pastoral hillside. Until 1955, when he visited England and America, the train that arrived at Malgudi station from the twentieth century had brought in only water tanks and electric power. Since then, the train to Malgudi had carried in, among other things, the dramatization of "The Guide."

I asked Narayan how he was getting on with his new book.

"I've been a little disturbed lately, so I haven't progressed very far," he said. "Instead of serious writing, I have been trying to do little pieces for *Vogue*, on such things as boredom and contentment and 'Are We Civilized?' " He had no theories about these assigned subjects, he added, but he thought some ideas might come to him somehow. "Will you have a betel nut?" he asked, handing me one. "Actually, I have been doing more reading than writing recently, and I have just stumbled upon a very good case for my sort of writing. You know, one or two critics are always attacking me for not having a style." From under a pile of groceries on the table he pulled a faded blue volume. It was edited by Forster and was called "Original Letters from India, 1779–1815." In his soft English, Narayan read some bits from Forster's introduction to Mrs. Eliza Fay's letters: " 'On one of her voyages a pair of globes accompanied her, but geography could never have been her strong point, for she thought the Alps were only one mountain thick, and the Malabar Hills the third highest range in the world. . . . Archdeacon Firminger observes with concern that "she frequently arranges her words in such an order that she

is bound to get into trouble with her relative pronouns."
She does. . . . And her mouth: how she does relish her
food! She is constantly registering through her senses,
and recording the results with . . . [an] untrained
mind. The outcome is most successful, and it is strange
that her letters are not better known in this country.
. . . Style is always being monopolized by the orderly-
minded; they will not admit that slap-dash people have
equal literary rights, provided they write slap-dash. If
Mrs. Fay got her relative pronouns correct she would be
a worse writer, for they can never have been correct in
her mind, she can never have spoken quite properly even
when calling at Government House or learning sweet
little Miss Rogers the use of the globes. She wrote as well
as she could, she wrote nothing that she herself was
not.' " After pausing a moment, Narayan said, "I say,
how beautifully Forster writes, doesn't he!"

When I left him, he was perched before his table,
which was crowded with nuts, herbs, rice, flour,
tomatoes, and onions.

1962

*1971. In the last nine years, Narayan has published
three books: "Gods, Demons, and Others" (1964), a re-
telling of Indian myths and legends; "The Vendor of
Sweets" (1967), a novel of father-son conflict in Malgudi; and "A Horse and Two Goats" (1970), a collection of short stories. The dramatization of "The Guide"
opened on Broadway in March, 1968, and closed after a
run of three days.*

VI

John Is Easy to Please

LINGUISTS ARE STIRRING UP QUITE A LOT OF intellectual dust just now with a theory of language known as transformational, or generative, grammar, which was first enunciated, in 1957, by Noam Chomsky, the leader of the linguistic vanguard, and which was recently denounced by Charles F. Hockett, a stalwart of the linguistic rearguard, as "a theory spawned by a generation of vipers." The two factions are polarized not only by rhetorical excess—Chomsky is a master of polemics in his own right—but also by actual issues, which are constantly being debated in the literature on the subject. Although Chomsky's two most influential books are "Syntactic Structures," which his disciples call the Old Testament, and "Aspects of the Theory of Syntax," which they call the New Testament, the clearest statement of the theory for someone unschooled in the technical jargon of transformational grammar is to be found in "Language and Mind," an expanded version of three lectures that Chomsky, a professor of linguistics at the Massachusetts Institute of Technology, gave in 1967 at the University of California at Berkeley. In the book, Chomsky took specific examples of grammatical rules relating to English phonology and syntax, and tried to demonstrate that their application was subject to certain universal conditions. These conditions, he argued, were the principles of "universal grammar" and provided "a highly restrictive schema to which any human language must conform." He wrote, "The study of universal grammar, so understood, is a study of the nature of human intellectual capacities. It tries to formulate the necessary and sufficient conditions that a system must meet to qualify as a potential human language, conditions that are not accidentally true to the existing human languages, but that are rather rooted in the human 'language capacity,' and thus constitute the innate organization that determines what counts as linguistic experience and what knowledge of language arises on the basis of this experience." He claimed that the human mind was equipped at birth with a mental representation of the universal grammar, and that this grammar, by means of formal operations he called "transformations," enabled a speaker of any language to generate an indefinite series of sentences. Indeed, he argued, the human mind was uniquely equipped to learn "natural" languages, and a child would fail to learn, as a first language, either the language of another planet or an artificial language that did not meet the universal conditions. Unlike earlier students of language, who had been content merely to describe usage, Chomsky hoped to discover and catalogue the conditions that he believed underlay not just usage but the acquisition of language. Venturing into philosophy, he revived the classic rationalist notion—first stated by Descartes in the seventeenth century—that certain ideas were implanted in the mind as innate equipment. In fact, for the purposes of his argument, he adopted the Cartesian distinction between mind, the essence of which was understanding and will, and body, the essence of which was extension and motion, and contended that the central problem on which Cartesianism foundered (If mind and body were separate substances, how did they interact in man?) could be solved through the study of language, for the creative use of language, the ability to produce and understand sentences, was what most obviously distinguished man from animal.

Chomsky alarmed many eminent philosophers by presenting his philosophical notions as basic to his theory of language. Two of these philosophers—Hilary Putnam and Nelson Goodman, both professors of philosophy at Harvard—tangled with Chomsky at a meeting impressively designated as the Innate Ideas Symposium of the American Philosophical Association and the Boston Colloquium for the Philosophy of Science, held in Boston in December, 1966. "What I would like to suggest is that contemporary research supports a theory of psychological *a priori* principles that bears a striking resemblance to the classical doctrine of innate ideas," Chomsky said at the Symposium. (Its proceedings were later published as a book, "Boston Studies in the Philosophy of Science," by the Humanities Press.) "We observe . . . that the tremendous intellectual accomplishment of language acquisition is carried out at a period of life when the child is capable of little else, and that this task is entirely beyond the capacities of an otherwise intelligent ape." Chomsky went on to describe the way he thought a child learned his first language: "Once a hypothesis—a particular grammar—is selected, the learner knows the language defined by this grammar; in particular, he is capable of pairing semantic and phonetic interpretations over an indefinite range of sentences to which he has never been exposed." Then Chomsky attacked the rationalists' historical adversaries—the empiricists and their modern successors, the behaviorists—who thought that the infant's mind was a clean slate and the infant's knowledge of language arose inductively from experience:

> We have a certain amount of evidence about the grammars that must be the output of an acquisition model. This evidence shows clearly that knowledge of language cannot arise by application of step-by-step inductive operations (. . . of association, conditioning, and so on) of any sort that have been developed or discussed within linguistics, psychology, or philosophy. Further empiricist speculations contribute nothing that even faintly suggests a way of overcoming the intrinsic limitations of the methods that have so far been proposed and elaborated. Furthermore [he laid his cards on the table], there are no other grounds for pursuing these empiricist speculations, and avoiding what would be the normal assumption, unprejudiced by doctrine, that one would formulate if confronted with empirical evidence of the sort sketched above. There is, in particular, nothing known in psychology or physiology that suggests that the empiricist approach is well-motivated, or that gives any grounds for skepticism concerning the rationalist alternative sketched above.

Putnam, rebuking Chomsky for littering his paper with fuzzy concepts, acknowledged some connection between grammar and linguistic behavior but pointed out that this connection was as little cause for recourse to innate ideas as was the connection between, say, a calculus textbook and mathematical intuition, or a drivers' manual and driving behavior. "How could something with *no* innate intellectual equipment *learn* anything?" he asked. (The italics here, as elsewhere, are from the sources.) *"To be sure,* human 'innate intellectual equipment' is relevant to language learning, if this means that such parameters as memory span and memory capacity play a crucial role. But what rank behaviorist is supposed to have ever denied *this?"* Putnam went on to contest the significance of certain features of Chomsky's "linguistic universals"—the bases of universal grammar. He observed that it was not remarkable that all languages should have nouns, for instance, since these were the most convenient way of specifying an object. Once the existence of nouns was granted, he believed, the existence of verbs followed of necessity. The existence of adjectives and adverbs—in fact, the existence of all parts of speech—was no more remarkable, and required no more special explanation, than the universal existence of numerals. Finally, Putnam attacked the foundation of Chomsky's theory of language— the notion that the human mind was "programmed" at birth to learn natural language, and was unable to learn bad or artificial language:

Suppose that language-using human beings evolved *independently* in two or more places. Then, if Chomsky were *right* there should be two or more *types* of human beings descended from the two or more original populations, and normal children of each type should fail to learn the languages spoken by the other types. Since we do not observe this, we have to conclude (if the I.H. [Innateness Hypothesis] is true) that language-using is an evolutionary "leap" that occurred only *once*. But in that case, it is overwhelmingly likely that all human languages are descended from a single original language, and that the existence today of what are called "unrelated" languages is accounted for by the great lapse of time and by countless historical changes. . . . But just this *consequence* of the I.H. is, in fact, enough to account for "linguistic universals"! For, if all human languages are descended from a common parent, then just such highly useful features of the common parent as the presence of some kind of quantifiers, proper names, nouns, and verbs, etc., would be expected to survive.

Putnam, who faulted Chomsky's theory point by point, at least did not make fun of it. But Goodman noted at the outset of his paper that Chomsky's was "a theory that only my respect for its advocate enables me to take at all seriously," and he went on to deliver his criticisms in the form of a Socratic dialogue between Jason (Chomsky), who had just returned from "Outer Cantabridgia," and Anticus (Goodman), who suspected that Jason had brought back a theory that was "more fleece than golden." Like Putnam, Goodman aimed his heaviest blows at Chomsky's notion that the human mind was uniquely equipped to learn natural language:

A [Anticus]: Can they [the linguists] really take an infant at birth, isolate it from all the influences of our language-bound culture, and attempt to inculcate it with one of the "bad" artificial languages?

J [Jason]: No. They readily admit this cannot be done. They regard their claim as a hypothesis not subject to such direct experimental test, but supported by ancillary considerations and evidence. . . .

A: Don't you think, Jason, that before anyone acquires a language, he has had an abundance of practice in developing and using rudimentary prelinguistic symbolic systems in which gestures and sensory and perceptual occurrences of all sorts function as signs? . . . When initial-language acquisition is seen as secondary-symbolic-system acquisition, the claim that there are rigid limitations upon initial-language acquisition is deprived of plausibility by the fact that there are no such limitations upon secondary-language acquisition. . . .

J: Does not all this just move the question back from the nature of languages that can be initially acquired to the nature of symbolic systems that can be so acquired? . . .

A: We'd certainly have an even harder time doing it. . . . Since the prelinguistic systems are likely to be fragmentary as well as rudimentary, we'd have trouble deciding when a system is acquired. And experimentation under all these difficulties would have to begin with symbol-using from the moment of birth. But I hardly have to refute your suspicions. Rather than facts crying for a theory, the theory is crying for the facts. . . . Inability to explain a fact does not condemn me to accept an intrinsically repugnant and incomprehensible theory. . . .

J: What is innate are not concepts, images, formulae, or pictures, but rather "inclinations, dispositions, habits, or natural potentialities." . . .

A: If all that is claimed is that the mind has certain inclinations and capacities, how can you justify calling these ideas? . . .

J: Again I am afraid I have not been careful enough. Rather than identify the innate ideas with capacities, etc., I probably should have said that these ideas exist as or are *"innate as"* such capacities.

A: A few minutes ago you accused me of sophistry; but I bow before the subtlety of that last statement. Go again, Jason, and bring back to me all the mysteries of ideas being innate as capacities. Then, if you like, we can talk again about unsubstantiated conjectures that cry for explanation by implausible and untestable hypotheses that hypostatize ideas that are innate in the mind as non-ideas.

A year and a half after the Innate Ideas Symposium, Chomsky did indeed return from a second voyage with "all the mysteries of ideas being innate as capacities," and the debate was resumed, this time at the ninth annual New York University Institute of Philosophy, the proceedings of which were later published as a book, "Language and Philosophy," by the New York University Press. The speakers at this conference included—in addition to Chomsky and Goodman—Reuben Abel, Raziel Abelson, Arthur Danto, Gilbert Harman, Sidney Hook, Paul Kurtz, Thomas Nagel, W. V. Quine, Leo Rauch, Robert Schwartz, Kenneth Stern, Rulon Wells, and Marvin Zimmerman. At the gathering, Chomsky tried to dispel some of the increasing suspicions of his critics. He dismissed Goodman's attack at the Innate Ideas Symposium with such scoffing remarks as "Given the dialogue form . . . it is difficult to be certain that one is not misrepresenting his [Goodman's] position" and "I do not see how to avoid the conclusion that when Goodman speaks of 'the unimpressive evidence adduced with respect to languages,' he simply speaks out of ignorance." For the most part, Chomsky merely answered his critics in terms of the very concepts they had criticized, and reasserted his ideas doggedly, as if his detractors had only misunderstood them.

Chomsky was knocked down repeatedly at conferences (the Innate Ideas Symposium and the New York University Institute of Philosophy were just two among many), and always seemed to return to the fray with greater confidence, his audience growing in the United States, in Europe, and beyond. In Britain, for instance, Chomsky matched wits with Stuart Hampshire, one of the best-known of the Oxford philosophers, on the B.B.C.'s Third Programme. Hampshire, like so many other modern philosophers, tried to make Chomsky see what it was that the philosophers regarded as obvious ambiguities in the doctrine of innate ideas. "I think a certain amount hinges, if one is to speak of innate ideas, on how abstract the transformations are," he remarked at one point, and he went on to say that if the transformations were not very abstract, they might simply be ordinary grammatical operations of a specific language, and if the transformations were very abstract, they might be so abstract that they could scarcely be said to constitute a universal grammar. He continued:

We have a traditional philosophical claim—the claim of empiricist philosophy . . . from the eighteenth century onwards—that language is learnt by association of ideas and by reinforcing responses, that concepts are formed in this way by abstraction, and that our grammar is a cultural phenomenon which varies with different cultures, with no common underlying structure and no necessity to prefer one structure to another; and then one has a contrary philosophical tradition [the rationalist one], that there are predispositions to form certain ideas and to organize concepts in a certain order, and even more strongly, that these ideas can be stated in a propositional form. The suggestion now is that a set of experiments, together with adequate statistical theory, show that one of these philosophical traditions [the empiricist one] was misguided and that the other—although we don't yet know how specific these abstract transformational principles are and whether they be anything like the traditional innate ideas—was correct. Is the conclusion you have reached one which is subject to controversy among others working in this field?

Chomsky replied that his conclusion was highly controversial, and Hampshire said:

The empiricist tradition . . . has always denied that there was anything that could be called innate ideas, meaning by this substantial propositions, beliefs as opposed to predispositions to behave in certain ways. Supposing one found that there were preferences for certain sound orders or word orders that really were very general, this might seem a feature of human behavior which in no way upsets the empiricist's picture—any more than it would if there was a predisposition to represent a scene on a piece of paper, given a pen, in a certain way. I suppose that the contrast here, which empiricists would insist on, would be between knowledge in the sense of propositional knowledge, which is said to be innate, and features of behavior, such as the tendency to represent on paper a solid body in a certain way, which may greatly vary culturally. Nonetheless, given all the possibilities there are of representation as something built-in, I don't see why empiricists should be upset by this feature of behavior, though they should be distressed if these predispositions amounted to something that could be called propositional knowledge or even to restricted categories of thought.

But Chomsky, instead of narrowing the scope of his theory under Hampshire's gently applied pressure, broadened it, saying:

Ability to acquire a language is not our only mental faculty, and I have no doubt that these other mental faculties also have their limitations. That there are such limitations would seem to me to follow from the fact that we are a biological organism. We can tell what a frog's limitations are, and some more complicated organism than us might be able to tell what our limitations are. I don't see that there's any contradiction in the idea that we could discover what our own limitations are in some fashion, but at the moment of course we can't get anywhere near that, except possibly in the case of certain artificially isolated components of the mind like the language faculty.

Hampshire bore down on the question of faculties:

You're making rather strong contrasts between the faculty that is exercised, say, in pure mathematics and the faculty that's exercised in recognizing and constructing new sentences. From the historical point of view, there's a certain paradox here if these two are separated too absolutely, because one would suppose that the logical structure and the linguistic argumentative structure have to be kept somehow under a single faculty.

Chomsky, seeing the philosophical trap, admitted that some of his claims were premature and required further study:

I think it would be dogmatic at the moment to take any position on this issue. All we can say is that we have evidence that the language faculty has such-and-such properties. We know for a fact that these properties are not a general limitation of human intelligence. . . . All right, so that just tells us that there are faculties beyond the language faculty. What the nature of those faculties [is], how they are interrelated to the language faculty—these are questions that have yet to be discovered by the study of other cognitive systems, by a study which may be analogous to the study of language.

One morning, I go to call on Chomsky at his office at M.I.T. It is in a run-down, sooty temporary structure put up during the Second World War. The office itself is a small, cramped room furnished with a couple of tables, a typewriter, and a few dilapidated chairs, and cluttered with papers and books. It could be an office in a factory. Chomsky sits in a chair of imitation leather (which is torn), typing furiously. He stands up to greet me, and smiles tentatively. He looks younger than his age, which is forty-two; indeed, he could easily pass for a graduate student. He is tall, with a long, thin nose in a long, thin face, and he has brown hair and brown eyes. He wears eyeglasses whose rims are dark at the top and clear at the bottom, and he is dressed in an old sweater and slacks. He clears some papers off a chair for me, and after we have settled down, I ask him how he happened to become interested in linguistics.

"I had a certain informal acquaintance with philology through my father, who is a scholar of Hebrew," he says. "He used to teach at Gratz College, a Hebrew teachers' college in Philadelphia; he now teaches at Dropsie College, a kind of graduate school of Semitic studies there. In fact, all his life he has been involved in Jewish education and Jewish culture. His main work is an important edition of the grammar of David Kimchi, which I read in proofs when I was eleven or twelve. But I began working on linguistics as an undergraduate at the University of Pennsylvania in the late forties for other reasons. I was thinking of dropping out of college, because I wanted to go to the Middle East to live on a kibbutz and work for Arab-Jewish coöperation—I was caught up in bi-nationalist alternatives to Zionism. I came under the influence of Zellig Harris, who was the star of the Linguistics Department at Penn. He had close ties to Israel from his childhood—his parents were Russian Jews, and he spent his early years in Palestine—and his academic background was in Semitic studies and linguistics. He shared my ideas on Zionism. Both of us were also involved in radical politics—I had passed through the various stages of Trotskyism and gone on to Marxist-Anarchist ideas. In any case, I started taking his courses, and got interested in linguistics."

When Chomsky is talking, he seems faintly surprised that anyone should like him. Although he hardly ever writes without touching off sparks, his manner in person is disarmingly modest, and although he has an air of youthful confidence, he is unassuming and friendly.

"As a teacher, Harris was unique," he continues. "He fitted all his teaching into one day a week, and he held many of his classes in the balcony of a Horn & Hardart's in Philadelphia, or at his apartment—in those days he lived first in New York and then in Princeton. Nowadays, he divides his time between Philadelphia and Israel, where his wife and child live on a kibbutz. I think he has a monthly commuter ticket on T.W.A." Chomsky breaks into a soft, shy smile. "In class, he always talked about the latest thing on his mind. He didn't pay any attention to what anybody else was doing in linguistics or in anything else, and I think his work suffered from that."

Chomsky has a slight cold, and keeps a box of Kleenex by his elbow. He takes a tissue and blows his nose.

"What is Harris's work like?" I ask.

"For as long as I have known Harris, he has been trying to work out formal analytic techniques that, in principle, could be applied by a computer to a corpus of linguistic data. While I was at Penn, he was trying to extend to longer discourses the techniques that he had developed with individual sentences. He wanted to be able to apply certain mechanical procedures to a text and find out the lines of argument, the reasoning and assumptions, behind the text—what was being said and what left unsaid. In order to apply his techniques to a text, he had to recast the sentences in parallel form and normalize them."

"What, exactly, do you mean by 'normalize'?" I ask.

"Say you had a text with the sentence 'England declared war,' and then, three lines down, the sentence 'War was declared by the Prime Minister,'" he says. "Well, Harris could do nothing with those two sentences, because they weren't parallel. But if you changed 'War was declared by the Prime Minister' to the active voice—that is, normalized it—then you got 'The Prime Minister declared war,' in which case 'England' and 'the Prime Minister' were in the same substitution class, the same theoretical frame: 'Blank declared war.' Then Harris could argue that with respect to this particular text 'England' and 'the Prime Minister' functioned in a similar fashion, although, of course, they didn't necessarily in the whole language. Reduced to its essentials, this was Harris's idea of normalization. Of course, his whole approach seems a little funny to me now, but as an undergraduate I was completely taken with it."

I ask him what kind of work he did in linguistics as an undergraduate.

"Next to Harris, I was most influenced by Nelson Goodman, who was at Penn then, and who was my philosophy teacher." He blows his nose again. "Though I don't think Harris and Goodman knew each other, they shared an intellectual attitude that I found exciting. What Goodman was trying to do in 'Structure of Appearance,' his great philosophical work, didn't seem so very different from what Harris was trying to do in linguistics. The most serious work I did as an undergraduate was to work out a grammar of modern Hebrew—my thesis. It turned out that by setting up very abstract models and looking for general principles I was able to get good theoretical explanations for many of the phenomena that modern linguistics, which in those days was mainly historical in approach, could only describe. The thesis contained the germs of my theory of transformational grammar."

I ask him when he made his break with Harris and went on to develop his own ideas.

"Goodman nominated me to the Society of Fellows at Harvard, and I became a Junior Fellow in 1951. At Harvard, I continued to work on Harris's kind of linguistics and on my transformational grammar as well. Eventually, I showed some of my work on transformational grammar to Morris Halle, who was an instructor here at M.I.T. then. He was very much excited by it, and told me to concentrate on it to the exclusion of everything else. I did, but the work was so unorthodox that at the end of my three-year term as a Junior Fellow no one would hire me as a linguist. The only job I could find was teaching Hebrew at Brandeis for twelve hours a week, at thirty-five hundred dollars a year. That was the last thing I wanted, so I stayed on at Harvard as a Junior Fellow for another year, and then Halle arranged for me to get an appointment to M.I.T. I had to do things like teaching elementary French and German to graduate students, because there was no Linguistics Department as such here at the time. In fact, until recently there were hardly any departments of linguistics in the country. Linguists were usually attached to anthropology, English, or foreign-language departments. The first large influx of money into linguistics came with the Second World War, when the Army set up language programs that were run by linguists. After the war, the field began exploding all over the place, and M.I.T., which began granting degrees in linguistics in 1961, has been at the forefront of linguistic progress. We've written papers on all kinds of topics." In one recent year, I later discover, the M.I.T. Linguistics Department produced such papers as "Some Languages That Are Not Context-Free," "Formal Justification of Variables in Phonemic Cross-Classifying Systems," "Theoretical Implications of Bloomfield's 'Menomini Morphophonemics,'" "Classes of Languages and Linear-Bounded Automata," "Vowel Harmony in Classical (Literary) Mongolian," "The Shift of 'S' to 'X' in Old Church Slavonic Verb Forms," and "Reduction of Long 'I' in Russian Imperative, Infinitive and Two Singular Morphemes."

"After you came to M.I.T., how were your ideas received in the academic world at large?" I ask.

"In the early years, I had a lot of trouble getting my work published. Eventually, Mouton, in The Hague, put out my books, but my ideas have always been too radical for the guild structure of the academic profession."

I ask him if his polemical bent had anything to do with the reception of his work.

"My ideas on both linguistics and politics are controversial, because they go to the root of the problem and give radical answers. Even before I came to M.I.T., I was told that my work would arouse much less antagonism if I didn't always couple my presentation of transformational grammar with a sweeping attack on empiricists and behaviorists and on other linguists. A lot of kind older people who were well disposed toward me told me

I should stick to my own work and leave other people alone. But that struck me as an anti-intellectual counsel. I believe that anything interesting involves a lot of guesswork and speculation, and anyone who is doing serious work in any field is going to be wrong an awful lot of the time. If he isn't, he's just a tragic bore. I know I've been wrong some of the time. In fact, I expect that my own theory will be incorporated one day in a new, perhaps richer theory, or be completely superseded."

I ask him who he thinks are the other major innovators in linguistics today.

"I don't know about other innovators, but there are a lot of transformationalists who I think are going to make good contributions in the future," he says. "Here at M.I.T., there is Morris Halle, who collaborated with me on 'The Sound Pattern of English,' and my former student John Ross."

I press my question. "Who would you say are the leading figures in the field as a whole, anywhere in the world?"

"There aren't any," he says, with a dismissive wave of the hand. "Most of the interesting work in linguistics is now being done here in the United States, and most of it is being done by transformationalists."

Although Chomsky is a student of language, his literary style is at once loose and pedantic. His sentences abound in awkward phrases ("Still more clearly to the point, I think") and are often ill-formed or weighted down with academic jargon ("No one took up Peirce's challenge to develop a theory of abduction, to determine those principles that limit the admissible hypotheses or present them in a certain order. Even today, this remains a task for the future. It is a task that need not be undertaken if empiricist psychological doctrine can be substantiated; therefore, it is of great importance to subject this doctrine to rational analysis, as has been done, in part, in the study of language"). He tends to lump people and concepts together indiscriminately ("Bloomfield, Bertrand Russell, positivistic linguists, psychologists, and philosophers in general"). Chomsky's style is characteristic of his school, and I ask him why it is that students of language have so little interest in style and so little sense of ordinary grammar.

"I assume that the writing in linguistics is no worse than the writing in any other academic field," he says. "The ability to use language well is very different from the ability to study it. Once, the Slavic Department at Harvard was thinking of offering Vladimir Nabokov an appointment. Roman Jakobson, the linguist, who was in the department then, said that he didn't have anything against elephants but he wouldn't appoint one a professor of zoology." Chomsky laughs.

I turn to Chomsky's politics. He has made a career of political radicalism, and yet in his books he often thanks agencies of the Defense Department for their financial support. For instance, the acknowledgments in "Syntactic Structures" read, "This work was supported in part by the U.S.A. Army (Signal Corps), the Air Force (Office of Scientific Research, Air Research and Development Command), and the Navy (Office of Naval Research); and in part by the National Science Foundation and the Eastman Kodak Corporation." I ask him why the Defense Department has supported his research.

"Ever since the Second World War, the Defense Department has been a main channel for the support of the universities, because Congress and society as a whole have been unwilling to provide adequate public funds," he says. "Luckily, Congress doesn't look too closely at the Defense Department budget, and the Defense Department, which is a vast and complex organization, doesn't look too closely at the projects it supports—its right hand doesn't know what its left hand is doing. Until 1969, more than half the M.I.T. budget came from the Defense Department, but this funding at M.I.T. is a bookkeeping trick. Although I'm a full-time teacher, M.I.T. pays only thirty to fifty per cent of my salary. The rest comes from other sources—most of it from the Defense Department. But I get the money through M.I.T."

I mention the protests in the spring of 1969 in which M.I.T. students demonstrated against certain aspects of the university's connection with the Defense Department.

"As a matter of fact, the trouble here then almost kept me from giving the John Locke Lectures at Oxford," he says. "The day before I was to leave for Oxford, I got a frantic telephone call from Robert Bishop, the Dean of Humanities and Social Science here. He asked me to call off the lectures and join the committee that had been appointed in response to the student protest against M.I.T.'s connection with the Defense Department. The Dean thought that my presence on the committee was essential to satisfy the radicals. I didn't want to call off the lectures, and the university wanted me to attend the weekly committee meetings, so they arranged to fly me back from England each week."

The entry under "labyrinth" in Webster's New International Dictionary (Second Edition) reads, in part:

(lăb´ĭ·rĭnth), n. [L. *labyrinthus*, fr. Gr. *labyrinthos*, fr. *labrys* double ax, prob. of Carian origin. cf. LABRYS.] 1. an edifice or place full of intricate passageways which render it difficult to find the way from the interior to the entrance, or from the entrance to the central compartment; a maze; specif. in Greek myth, the labyrinth constructed by Daedalus for Minos, king of Crete, in which the Minotaur was confined.

The mythical labyrinth was, according to one authority, "so artfully contrived that whoever was enclosed in it could by no means find his way out unassisted," and another has written, "Once inside one would go endlessly along its twisting paths without ever finding the exit. . . . In whatever direction they ran the victims might be running straight to the monster; if they stood still he might at any moment emerge from the maze." As every schoolboy knows, these victims were Athenian youths and maidens sent as tribute to Crete, where they were fed to the Minotaur, who was half man and half bull. When the great Athenian hero Theseus was sent to Crete as part of the tribute, Minos's daughter Ariadne fell in love with him and furnished him with a ball of thread to enable him to escape from the labyrinth. Theseus fastened one end of the thread to the inside of the door to the labyrinth and unwound the ball as he went along the twisted passages, until he came upon the

Minotaur. He killed the Minotaur, and escaped from the labyrinth by following the thread back to the door.

After spending some time with Chomsky's works on linguistics, I discover that he has all the ingenuity of a Daedalus, so I take a big ball of thread with me when I go to meet him for the second time. I step through the door of his office and boldly ask him to explain transformational grammar.

"The traditional multi-volume grammars that you find on the shelves of libraries present and classify precisely the examples that appear in them, and nothing else," he says. "But we transformationalists try to answer the mysterious and, I think, rather profound question: What qualities of intelligence does a human being possess that make it possible for him to use language creatively, to generate from the limited set of examples that he hears an infinite set of sentences? But perhaps the clearest way to explain the theory of transformational grammar is to show how transformations operate in sentences. Sentences consist of phrases of various types—noun phrases, verb phrases, adverbial phrases, and so on. O.K.? For purposes of analysis, every sentence can be enclosed within brackets, and its parts enclosed within smaller brackets and marked, and the parts of the parts enclosed within still smaller brackets and marked, and so on. O.K.? You end up with a sentence that's properly bracketed, or parenthesized, in the technical sense that every left parenthesis is associated with a right parenthesis and the entire structure is exhausted at every stage of the analysis. Take the sentence 'John kept the car that was in the garage.' " From my reading, I recognize the sentence as a variation of one of Chomsky's stock examples, "John kept the car in the garage." "It consists of the noun phrase—in this case, really a noun—'John'; the verb 'kept'; and the noun phrase 'the car that was in the garage.' O.K.? The noun phrase 'the car that was in the garage' consists, in turn, of the noun 'car' and the sentence 'that was in the garage'; the shorter sentence 'that was in the garage' consists, in turn, of other phrases; and so on. O.K.? The whole sentence can be bracketed and labelled with abbreviations—sentence, noun phrase, noun, verb phrase, verb, article, and so on."

He diagrams the sentence on a sheet of paper:

$$\left[\begin{array}{c}\left[\text{John}\right]\end{array}\right]_{S \; N \; N}\quad\left[\begin{array}{c}\left[\text{kept}\right]\end{array}\right]_{VP \; V \; V \; NP}\left[\begin{array}{c}\left[\text{the}\right]\left[\text{car}\right]\end{array}\right]_{NP \; Art \; Art \; N \; N \; NP}$$

$$\left[\begin{array}{c}\left[\left[\text{that}\right]\right]\end{array}\right]_{S \; NP \; N \; N \; NP \; VP}\left[\left[\text{was}\right]\right]_{V \; V \; PP}\left[\left[\text{in}\right]\right]_{P \; P \; NP}\left[\left[\text{the}\right]\right]_{Art \; Art}$$

$$\left[\text{garage}\right]_{N \quad N \; NP \; PP \; VP \; S \; NP \; VP \; S}$$

"Now, the fundamental idea of transformational grammar is that the bracketed and labelled representation of a sentence is its surface structure, and associated with each sentence is a long sequence of more and more abstract representations of the sentence—we transformationalists call them phrase markers—of which surface structure is only the first," he continues. "For example, underlying the surface structure of 'John kept the car that was in the garage,' which might be represented by the phrase marker P_1, there would be, embedded and unspoken, a somewhat more abstract phrase marker, P_2, which would be converted into P_1 by what we call a transformation, transformation being our term for the operation by which less abstract phrase markers are generated from more abstract ones. And underlying P_2 would be a still more abstract phrase marker, P_3, which would be converted into P_2 by another transformation, and so on, back farther and farther, until you reach the most abstract phrase marker of all, which we call the deep structure of the sentence. Whereas the surface structure in general is not closely related to the meaning of the sentence, the deep structure appears to be closely related to meaning. O.K.?"

As Chomsky talks, he radiates feverish intensity. His cheeks become flushed, and his hands fly back and forth to underscore his points.

"Is it really the case that the meaning of the sentence is hidden in this complicated way?" I ask.

"Keep the old sentence, 'John kept the car that was in the garage,' in the back of your mind for now and let me give you the simpler sentence 'John kept the car in the garage' as an example of what I mean. O.K.? Notice that 'John kept the car in the garage' is ambiguous—is open to two interpretations. Call them I_1 and I_2. I_1 would be exactly the same as 'John kept the car that was in the garage'; you could paraphrase this interpretation as 'It was the car in the garage that John kept.' I_2 would be 'The car was kept in the garage by John'; you could paraphrase this interpretation as 'It was in the garage that John kept the car.' Although you can't tell by the sound of the sentence which of the two interpretations is meant, the surface structure of the sentence is different for each interpretation. When we follow interpretation I_1, 'It was the car in the garage that John kept,' we assume that the phrase 'the car in the garage' is a unit, bracketed as a noun phrase."

He diagrams the phrase on the sheet of paper:

$$\left[\text{the car in the garage}\right]$$
$$NP \qquad\qquad\qquad NP$$

"But when we follow interpretation I_2, 'It was in the garage that John kept the car,' then we assume that 'the car in the garage' is not a unit, not a noun phrase," he continues. "Instead, 'the car' is a full noun phrase—"

He diagrams:

$$\left[\text{the car}\right]$$
$$NP \qquad NP$$

"—and 'in the garage' is an adverbial phrase—"
He diagrams:

$$\left[\text{in the garage}\right]$$
$$Adv\ P \qquad\qquad Adv\ P$$

"According to the interpretation I₁, 'John kept the car in the garage' is an elliptical form of the explicit, and more abstract, sentence 'John kept the car that was in the garage,'" he continues. "The surface structure is generated from the more abstract sentence by the transformation that deletes the words 'that was.' Ellipsis, a linguistic term that was in use long before the advent of transformational grammar, is one kind of operation that transforms one phrase marker into another. The abstract phrase marker 'John kept the car that was in the garage' itself derives from a deeper, more explicit sentence— 'John kept the car. The car was in the garage.'"

He diagrams:

$$\left[{}_S\left[{}_N\left[{}_N \text{John}\right]\right]\left[{}_{VP}\left[{}_V\left[{}_V \text{kept}\right]\right]\left[{}_{NP}\left[{}_{NP}\left[{}_{Art}\left[{}_{Art}\text{the}\right]\right]\left[{}_N\left[{}_N\text{car}\right]\right]\right]\right.\right.\right.$$

$$\left[{}_S\left[{}_{NP}\left[{}_{Art}\left[{}_{Art}\text{the}\right]\right]\left[{}_N\left[{}_N\text{car}\right]\right]\right]\left[{}_{VP}\left[{}_V\left[{}_V\text{was}\right]\right]\left[{}_{PP}\left[{}_P\left[{}_P\text{in}\right]\right]\left[{}_{NP}\left[{}_{Art}\left[{}_{Art}\text{the}\right]\right.\right.\right.\right.\right.$$

$$\left.\left[{}_N\left[{}_N\text{garage}\right]\right]\right]_{NP}\Big]_{PP}\Big]_{VP}\Big]_S\Big]_{NP}\Big]_{VP}\Big]_S$$

I feel I am being drawn deeper and deeper into the intricacies of Chomsky's theory, but the explanation is so lucid (no doubt Chomsky has delivered it often) that I still have my bearings.

"This sentence brings us almost to the deep structure, which in the case we've been talking about, as it happens, is not very abstract," he goes on. "Now let's take a more complex example, the interrogative sentence 'What did John keep the car in?' We transformationalists would argue that this sentence derives from an underlying, more abstract sentence, 'John kept the car in the garage'—in which 'the car' is the noun phrase and 'in the garage' is an adverbial phrase—not by an operation of ellipsis this time but, rather, by the operations of substitution and pre-positioning, which substitute 'what' for 'garage' and move 'what' to the beginning of the sentence. These transformations yield the phrase 'what John kept the car in,' which, in turn, is transformed by further operations into the sentence 'What did John keep the car in?' "

I am beginning to lose my way. I ask him about the universal conditions that are supposed to govern transformations, and he tells me that although the sentence "John kept the car in the garage" is ambiguous, the question "What did John keep the car in?" is not ambiguous, for it is open to only one interpretation—"It was in the garage that John kept the car."

"Why is it that the question is not ambiguous?" he asks rhetorically. "Well, we transformationalists would say that the question 'What did John keep the car in?' is governed by a universal condition—undoubtedly a principle of universal grammar—that asserts that a noun phrase, here 'the garage,' that is part of a larger noun phrase, here 'the car in the garage,' cannot be extracted and moved. Thus, from the sentence 'John kept the car that was in the garage' I cannot form the question 'What did John keep the car that was in?' That would be impossible in any language. O.K.? When we take interpretation I_1 of the sentence 'John kept the car in the garage,' in which 'the car in the garage' is a noun phrase, we cannot extract the phrase 'the garage' and put it in the front and form a question. But, as you noticed, when we take interpretation I_2, in which 'in the garage' is an adverbial phrase, then we can substitute 'what' for 'the garage,' move 'what' to the front of the sentence, and get 'What did John keep the car in?' O.K.? This is an example of a rather non-trivial point—that in order to form questions the speaker of a language, in this case English, applies transformations such as the operations of substitution and pre-positioning to mental representations of declarative sentences. Because these mental representations are a sequence of phrase markers, the speaker has to know, in order to produce and understand sentences, the underlying structures of the sentences to which he is applying the transformations. He has to know, for example, whether the phrase marker to which he applies the transformation treated 'the car in the garage' as a single noun phrase or whether it treated 'the car' as a noun phrase and 'in the garage' as an adverbial phrase.''

"I don't quite grasp the distinction between the grammatical rules of transformation that you were speaking about before and these universal conditions,'' I say.

"An example of a grammatical rule of transformation

would be the rule of question formation that I gave you," he says. "Let me clarify it further. Take the declarative sentence 'John read the book.' If I want to form a question about the book, I move the phrase 'the book' to the beginning of the sentence and prefix the questioning element 'what,' and I get 'What book did John read?' "

"Don't you actually get 'What the book did John read?' " I ask.

"That was a bad example, because it brings up complexities in the rule of question formation that I would just as soon not go into now," he says, and he presses on. "This grammatical rule of question formation can be applied to any noun phrase in the sentence. If I want to form a question about John, instead of the book, I say, 'Who read the book?' "

"Actually, 'Who John read the book?' " I ask.

"That was a bad example, too. But, to go on, all grammatical rules of transformation, like the rule of question formation, must meet certain universal conditions. One such universal condition, as you noticed, is that no grammatical rule of transformation can involve extracting a noun phrase from another noun phrase that properly includes it—'the car' from 'the car in the garage.' "

I try to draw him away from examples by asking him how he regards the workings of these rules and conditions. "Surely they are not conscious?" I say.

"In the normal use of the language, we unconsciously and instantaneously make use of abstract representations," he says.

"If these rules and conditions are in fact unconscious, then why think of them in formal terms as structures—as mental representations?" I ask.

"Let me answer your question in this way," he says. "Take two examples somewhat more complex than the sentences we've been talking about: 'John is eager to please' and 'John is easy to please.' O.K.?" I immediately recognize these sentences as the most famous examples of Chomsky's school. "We could assign to these two sentences their respective surface structures—a noun, 'John,' followed by a verb, 'is,' followed by a certain kind of adjective phrase, 'eager to please' in one case, 'easy to please' in the other. But the surface structures don't tell the whole story. If we say 'John is eager to please,' 'John' is the subject of 'please'—John is doing the pleasing. We attribute to John the property of being eager to do something. Now, if we say 'John is easy to please,' 'John' is the direct object of 'please.' We mean that pleasing John is easy and we attribute to the proposition 'please John' the property of being easy. O.K.? Although the two sentences differ considerably in the grammatical relation between their parts—in what is predicated of what—these differences are not represented in their surface structures. In the case of 'John is eager to please,' the surface structure and the deep structure are really identical—that 'John' is the subject of 'please' is already explicit in the surface structure. But in the case of 'John is easy to please' the surface structure, 'John is easy to please,' is quite different from the deep structure, 'To please John is easy' or 'For us to please John is easy,' and it requires a long sequence of operations to transform this deep structure into its surface structure. I won't try to explain all these transformations now, because they're a little too complicated. But in the deep structure of 'John is easy to please' the verb-object relation between 'to please' and 'John' is explicit, whereas in the surface structure the relation is not explicit at all. It is possible, however, to conceive of a surface structure for this particular meaning—the meaning 'To please John is easy'—in which the verb-object relationship between 'John' and 'to please' would be explicit. This would be true for the surface structure 'To please John is easy.' To transform the deep structure 'To please John is easy' into the surface structure 'To please John is easy' involves only the simplest of operations."

"But in another language—say, in French or Latin—wouldn't the difference between what is predicated of what in 'John is eager to please' and in 'John is easy to please' be expressed by the case of the noun, or by the addition of a preposition?" I ask. "If so, then what you speak of as the contrast between the deep structures and the identity of the surface structures of these two sentences might be relevant only to English."

"Yes," he says. "In French or Latin, the surface structures of the two sentences would certainly not be identical, but the two surface structures would still show greater similarity to each other than the two deep structures would. O.K.? In French or Latin, these sentences would retain in their surface structures things like cases, which are a sort of residual deep structure. But in English they don't, so you get an amusing and striking example of sentences whose surface structures are identical but whose deep structures are radically different."

"But does the contrast between 'John is eager to please' and 'John is easy to please' actually matter to someone using English?" I ask.

"The real contrast between the two sentences shows up in the way in which we perform certain syntactic operations on them, like the operation of nominalization," he says. "If we have the sentence 'John is weak,' we can perform the operation of nominalization and produce the noun phrase 'John's weakness.' If we have 'John is eager to please,' by the same operation we can produce the noun phrase 'John's eagerness to please.' But if we perform the same operation on 'John is easy to please,' we produce 'John's easiness to please.' This is not a properly formed noun phrase. You can say 'John's eagerness to please surprised me,' but you can't say 'John's easiness to please surprised me.' If somebody said it, you would know what he meant, but you would also know that he didn't know how to speak English properly. Thus, the contrast between 'John is eager to please' and 'John is easy to please' appears as a difference in grammaticality when we perform the operation of nominalization. This simple example illustrates the fact that when we perform certain operations, we perform them not on actual sentences but on mental representations, on the sequences of abstract structures that underlie sentences. For what we transformationalists are saying is that grammar is really in the mind—that it is a fixed, finite set of internalized rules and conditions which associates the surface structures of sentences with particular sounds and particular meanings and makes it possible for the speaker of a language to generate an infinite number of sentences."

I ask him what he thinks the relationship between sound and meaning is.

"It has to do with the phonological, syntactic, and semantic components of grammar that form the framework of our theory. Transformationalists are divided over the precise boundaries of these components, but my view is that the phonological component assigns, among other things, an intonational structure—a stress and pitch contour—to each surface structure. For example, the phrase 'lighthouse keeper,' meaning the keeper of a lighthouse, would be bracketed one way—"

A diagram:

$$\left[\begin{matrix} \left[\begin{matrix} \left[\text{light} \right] & \left[\text{house} \right] \\ A \ \ A & N \ \ N \end{matrix} \right] & \left[\text{keeper} \right] \\ N & N \ \ N \end{matrix} \right]$$

"—and the phrase 'light housekeeper,' meaning a housekeeper who isn't a heavy person, would be bracketed in a different way."

Another diagram:

$$\left[\begin{matrix} \left[\text{light} \right] & \left[\begin{matrix} \left[\text{house} \right] & \left[\text{keeper} \right] \\ N \ \ N & N \ \ N \end{matrix} \right] \\ A \ \ A & N \end{matrix} \right]$$

"In the first instance 'lighthouse' is a lexical unit, in the second instance 'housekeeper' is a lexical unit, and when we hear these two phrases, which have different stress and pitch contours, we mentally reconstruct their surface structures. In fact, we rely upon an abstract representation to interpret even the simplest words we hear. Take the words 'explain' and 'explanation.' It's obvious that they are almost identical, so there has to be a single underlying representation for them."

"Does that really follow?" I ask, unwinding my skein.

"Yes," he says. "On the more abstract level, it has to be true. But, to go on, the sound pattern of 'explanation' is rather different from the sound pattern of 'explain.' If the same sound pattern appeared in both cases, we would say 'explain' and 'explain-ation.' Instead, we say 'explain' and 'explanation,' because in 'explanation' the vowels and the stress have changed. These changes are determined by phonological rules."

"But when you discuss 'explain' and 'explanation' in terms of an underlying form, aren't you violating your own definition of the phonological component—that it connects only surface structure and sound?" I ask, trying, for the sake of understanding, to think in the jargon of transformational grammar.

" 'Explain' and 'explanation' is actually a bad example, because it brings up certain theoretical notions that I don't want to go into here," he says. "But the phonological component does relate the physical event to the surface structure, and that brings me to the syntactic component. When we know the surface structure of a sentence, the syntactic component comes into operation and assigns to the surface structure a syntactic derivation, a sequence of phrase markers that, as I have described, begins with the surface structure and ends with the deep structure. For example, the sentence 'John is easy to please' would have this surface structure—"

A diagram:

$$\left[\ \left[\text{John}\right]_N\ \right]_N\ \left[\ \left[\text{is}\right]_V\ \left[\ \left[\text{easy}\right]_A\ \left[\text{to please}\right]_A\ \right]_{VP}\ \right]_{VP}\ \right]_{AP}\ _{VP}\ \right]_S$$

$$_S\quad N\quad N\quad VP\quad V\quad V\quad AP\quad A\quad A\quad VP\quad VP\quad AP\quad VP\quad _S$$

"—and certain intermediate structures, which I won't go into, and what is roughly the deep structure, 'To please John is easy.' From this deep structure, our third component—the semantic component—draws the grammatical relations that are relevant to the interpretation of the sentence, and assigns a meaning to the sentence. In the case of 'John is easy to please,' the semantic component interprets the sentence as predicating for pleasing John the property of being easy."

Some of the distinctions have begun to seem blurred and elusive. For instance, is deep structure the meaning, or different from meaning? When Chomsky is discussing syntax, he sometimes seems to treat the two terms as synonyms, but when he is discussing semantics, he seems to contrast them. I tell him about my confusion.

"We transformationalists are at very different stages in our understanding of the three components," he says, with a smile. "I think we are at quite an advanced stage in our understanding of the phonological component; we have fairly substantial insight into the way surface structure is graphed onto sound, and we can formulate and order hundreds of phonological rules. We are still at a rudimentary stage in our understanding of the syntactic component, and we have practically no understanding of the semantic component—no one has even been able to devise a really good terminology for the semantic representation of sentences, let alone the rules that apply to them. At the moment, semantic representation is pretty much a dream."

The whole idea of components seems to me quite remote and arbitrary, and I wonder if they have any basis in experience. "Have you done any experiments with children to learn how they acquire language?" I ask.

"No. I hate experiments."

"Has your distaste for experiments played any part in your thinking about linguistics?"

"I think that even without doing any experiments you can deduce some pretty striking things about what must be happening in the infant's mind. The infant must know the rules and conditions of grammar before he learns a language. After acquiring a rudimentary knowledge of a language, he observes the linguistic data and asks himself, 'Are the linguistic data that I'm presented with consistent with the hypothesis that this is, for example, English?' And then he says to himself, 'Yes, it is English. O.K., then, I know this language.' In time, he is able to use the full range of knowledge that is expressed by the grammar of English. The problem of determining whether what he's presented with is in fact English, rather than, say, Japanese, is a far simpler problem than the problem of creating a knowledge of English from the partial and degenerate linguistic data with which he's presented. Now, I don't mean all this to be taken very literally, but it seems to me that, as a rough first approximation, my idea that the infant acquires a language through the formulation of hypotheses that he checks against the linguistic data is probably a better characterization of learning than the empiricist one or the modern behaviorist one. As for experiments, I think that people can do them later to fill in the details and verify the theory."

"By the way, do you have children of your own?" I ask.

"Yes, Carol and I have three children," he says.

"By one estimate, there are about four thousand languages spoken today, and there must have been many more in the past, some of which have probably left no trace at all," I observe. "How can you verify your universal theory without a knowledge of quite a number of them?"

"It is true that we transformationalists have studied only a handful of languages in a really intensive way, but each new language that we study intensively in the future will support the conclusions that we have already drawn. I'm confident of this, because it seems to me that if we assume that any infant can learn any language—that no infant is genetically a speaker of a specific language—then every attribute we postulate in order to explain an infant's ability to learn one language must be true of any child's learning of any language, and so must be a universal condition of a universal grammar. Thus, on the basis of the evidence that we have from the study of a few languages we can safely assume that for learning languages there must be a schematism in the mind—a physical mechanism in the brain—that is the same in every human being."

At random, I pick one of the many objections that occur to me, and ask him whether, if there is an actual mechanism in the brain, it wouldn't be better if the neurosurgeons located it before the linguists drew conclusions from its existence.

"Neurophysiology is in too primitive a state now to find the mechanism. For them, it's just a dream. We linguists hope to show the neurophysiologists what to look for."

I bring up certain criticisms of Chomsky's school that are persistently made by other linguists: that the structures, operations, and components—all the abstract models and analytical apparatus—of transformational grammar have little relation to language as it is actually used; that although Chomsky and his followers claim that they arrive at their conclusions by the scientific method, their approach is in the main deductive and scholastic; and that language is by nature rough and confused, and does not have any hard and fast rules.

"What all those criticisms of our work really come down to is whether we ought to be studying transformational grammar at all or doing something else," he says. "What really bugs these critics is that we construct an idealization of language and then study it. But this is a criticism of every kind of intellectual activity and could be applied to the procedures of any science."

"Is that really the case? Surely there are many kinds of intellectual activity that don't involve what you call 'idealization.' Anyway, couldn't it be that the study of language calls for a very different approach from the study of natural science?"

"Yes, that's conceivable, but I don't believe it. Some intellectuals think that in certain fields of study all you can say is: I saw this and then I saw that and then I saw some other thing. They say that these fields are not subject to scientific investigation. But that's just a counsel of despair, and there isn't the slightest reason to believe it, particularly in the case of language. If our approach doesn't make sense, then there is no point in studying language at all. Think of the computer as a model for the human mind. A scientist who didn't know what the program, or input, of the computer was would assume that the only way to find it out would be to analyze the output, language. He would construct an idealization, a model, and develop an explanatory theory in the hope that in time he would be able to deduce the input. If there was some screw loose in the computer, then the output would not be the result of the input, and the scientist would never be able to deduce the input—what he took to be the input would really be the result of a mechanical quirk. But if there was not a screw loose in the computer, then the scientist would be right in his assumption. In fact, his way would be the only way to discover the input."

The computer analogy seems to me to be somewhat misleading, especially since it takes for granted some of Chomsky's fairly controversial opinions about the human mind. The trouble is that Chomsky's discussions of language always seem to draw him toward larger issues of philosophy, psychology, and scientific method, and his views on these questions are sketchy and diffuse. "When you're dealing with sentences and examples from linguistics, your ideas seem more systematic than when you're dealing with other subjects," I remark. "Is that an unfair assumption?"

"No, that's very fair, I think. Of course, one could study technical linguistics for itself, but, for as long as I can remember, it has been big, ultimate philosophical questions that have made my technical work seem worthwhile to me. I especially want to know if the human brain comes, in a sense, initially informed as to the nature of the knowledge that it's going to acquire later. I suspect that we even have some innate equipment for processing certain kinds of physical, phenomenal entities, such as faces. I think that, just as we have abstract deep structures which are transformed into speech by a long series of mental operations, and which we use to interpret speech, so we may also have an abstract characterization of the human face which is superimposed on various physical events through a relatively long series of projections, and which we use to interpret the variant manifestations of the face. We may recognize a face from different angles because, at the level of deep structure, the face is represented by a single mental entity."

He is off again on his pet theory of structures, and I ask weakly, "Couldn't it be a mental image of the face?"

"The example of language leads me to believe that abstract representations of physical phenomena are typical of human intelligence. In fact, I think that we have abstract representations for everything—for the world, for our system of beliefs about the world, for personal relationships, and so on."

"Is there anything that worries you at present about the theory of transformational grammar?" I ask.

"No," he says. "I don't think there could be. If one doesn't like vague talk about language, then one automatically arrives at something like the theory of transformational grammar, and the problem becomes one of refining the theory. But the dominant movement in this century has been and still is structural linguistics. In fact, Harris, who I think was the first to use the term 'transformation,' is essentially a structuralist. He would dismiss deep structure as a mythical invention, because for him transformations are not operations on common, abstract deep structures but only a means of normalizing sentences. He thinks, for instance, that an active sentence is merely a manipulation of its passive."

I stand up, and so does he.

"I should perhaps add that in Harris's work, and in the work of some others, there are occasional vague hints that one might have to account for something beyond the observed data, such as new, unfamiliar sentences," he says. "For the most part, however, structural linguists think that new sentences are formed by analogy, blending, and editing. But the minute you formalize these concepts, you discover that they're only hand-waving. When you first hear the unfamiliar sentence 'John is easy to please,' how do you know that it's not analogous to the familiar sentence 'John is eager to please'? They certainly seem analogous. Actually, of course, they are not analogous, because 'John is easy to please' really means someone else is going to do the pleasing of John but 'John is eager to please' really means that John is going to do the pleasing. Transformational grammar offers the only possible explanation for features like the creative and elliptical qualities of language."

On another occasion, Chomsky tells me, "Of course, I'm prejudiced, but I think the structuralist approach to language is fundamentally taxonomic. Its most basic techniques for arriving at what the structuralists consider a grammar are segmentation and classification. Let me explain. Say you're the informant, a speaker of English, and I'm the linguist, who doesn't speak English. I point to a small, furry animal asleep in the corner of this office, and you make a noise. I write the noise down phonetically as 'k-h-a-t'—'h' because I hear a burst of air after your 'k.' I just write it down blindly. I don't know whether or not the noise means anything in your language. I collect a lot of data in this manner, and in due course I observe that every time a 'k' occurs at the beginning of your utterance it is followed by an 'h.' I conclude that 'k-h' must be a single phonetic segment, a single unit of noise. Later, however, I observe that when you make a noise like 'scat,' you don't have a burst of air after the sound 'k.' I conclude that 'k' is a phoneme, the smallest significant unit of sound, and that it has a burst of air after it when it begins a word and no burst of air when it follows an 's.' I further observe that these two noises are in what's called complementary distribution. That is, in any context only one of them is possible; one never finds 'k-h' occupying in one word the same position that 'k' occupies in another. After I have catalogued a lot of phonemes in this manner, I begin to classify them. I observe which phonemes occur before 'a-t'—'p,' 'b,' 't,' and so on. I observe that 'eh' never occurs before '-at;' there is no such word as 'ehat.' so I call phonemes that can precede the sound 'at' without altering it consonants. I proceed in this manner with different segments of your utterances, and I observe that certain sequences of phonemes occur in a regular way. 'Khat,' which has three phonemes, occurs in a lot of places and in similar ways. I conclude that 'khat' is a morpheme, the minimal meaning-bearing unit. I follow the same procedure with morphemes that I followed with phonemes, and I observe that 'slept' and 'sleep' are two variants of a single morpheme, because one, 'slep,' occurs only before 't,' and the other, 'sleep,' occurs only in isolation. I therefore set up an abstract morpheme of which 'slept' and 'sleep' are two manifestations. I go on to develop categories of morphemes, such as nouns and verbs. Then I look at certain possible sequences of these categories—such as article-noun, 'the cat,' and article-adjective-noun, 'the sleeping cat'—and I keep going until I arrive at the notion of a sentence. The record of all the segments and all the categories, all the data that I have collected—that record is my grammar."

The greatest exponent of structural linguistics in the United States was Leonard Bloomfield, who lived from 1887 to 1949. He studied Algonquian, Malayo-Polynesian, and Indo-European languages, especially Germanic phonology and morphology, but he is best remembered for his book "Language," an attempt to synthesize the science of linguistics. In an obituary for Bloomfield, the Yale linguist Bernard Bloch wrote:

> In his long campaign to make a science of linguistics, the chief enemy that Bloomfield met was that habit of thought which is called mentalism: the habit of appealing to mind and will as ready-made explanations of all possible problems. Most men regard this habit as obvious common sense; but in Bloomfield's view, as in that of other scientists, it is mere superstition, unfruitful at best and deadly when carried over into scientific research. In the opposite approach—known as positivism, determinism, or mechanism—Bloomfield saw the main hope of the world; for he was convinced that only the knowledge gained by a strictly objective study of human behavior, including language, would one day make it possible for men to live at peace with each other.

The most prominent of Bloomfield's living disciples is Charles Hockett, who with the publication of "The State of the Art," in 1968, established himself as Chomsky's most vocal critic as well. Hockett teaches at Cornell, and I meet him by arrangement at his house in Ithaca. It is a large prefabricated, Techbuilt structure, with a lot of glass.

"The Techbuilt process is one of the few good things to come out of M.I.T.," Hockett tells me as he takes me into the living room. He is a big, solid-looking man in his mid-fifties, with slightly tinted dark-gray hair, a slightly tinted dark-gray goatee, and dark-blue eyes. He wears dark-rimmed glasses and smokes a pipe. He is dressed in a dark-gray suit, a plaid shirt, a bright tie, and slippers. He excuses himself for a moment and turns off a record of a piece of atonal music that has been playing loudly in another room. The living room is light and airy, and is furnished in a fairly modern style. There is a grass-green carpet, a piano, and chairs and a long sectional sofa upholstered in a black-and-brown pattern, and around the room are the mementos of a traveller—American Indian masks, a large brass tray from southern India, a tapa cloth from the South Pacific.

"I always work with the stereo system going," Hockett says as he rejoins me.

He lights his pipe, and I explain my interest in linguistics and ask him to tell me about Bloomfield.

Hockett puffs at his pipe for a while. Then he says abruptly, "That's a tall order. I studied with him in Chicago for a couple of quarters after I finished my Ph.D. But he usually affected people more through his writings than through his personality, which was gentle and unassuming, though he did have a pixyish sense of humor." Hockett's voice rises in pitch, as if to emphasize his sincerity, as he continues, "His death was a great loss to linguistics. He was the last of the great linguists. The field is now aswarm with locusts—terrorized by transformationalists. Their studies are as worthless as horoscopes. It's a shame, but I think that many of the young transformationalists, who are intelligent, have sold their birthright of scholarship for a mess of pottage. I don't object to letting Chomsky and Halle teach all the transformational theory they want, but these young kids should also be given some grounding in traditional linguistics, if for no other reason than that they need some basis for comparison."

His manner of speaking is deliberate and somewhat portentous, with sudden changes in thought. Listening to him, one imagines that he is a little intimidating to his students.

I ask him if he thinks that Chomsky and his school have made any contribution at all to linguistics.

He is again slow to answer, but finally says, "Given the avidity with which some of the younger transformationalists are applying themselves, one has to concede that their approach is revealing some interesting things about English syntax. The notion of working by ordered rules from underlying forms to spoken forms is very nice indeed, but the transformationalists confuse the machinery of analysis with the object being analyzed. They claim that these underlying forms exist independently of their investigations. That's tripe. They are only convenient tools. To take a simple case, in English the plural of 'boy' is made with a 'z' sound and the plural of 'cat' is made with an 's' sound. You can invent an underlying form to include 'z' and 's,' and make rules that will tell you when the plural of a noun should be pronounced with a 'z' and when with an 's'—and, for that matter, when with an 'e-s.' But you must always keep in mind that although 'z' and 's' are intrinsic to the language, the hunk of stuff—the underlying form—is something that you have brought in for your own convenience."

I ask him if he thinks that personalities are an issue in the dispute between Chomsky's school and the structural linguists.

"It's always easy to slide off from a discussion of issues to a dissection of personalities. In print, I try to avoid imputing idiocy or evil, knavery or foolery to the transformationalists. But before I reach print I am apt to let myself go. In an early draft of 'The State of the Art,' I tossed quite a lot of snide insults at the transformationalists and took a few cracks at Chomsky. I sent the draft to Bill Bright, the editor of *Language*, for his consideration. I neglected to tell him not to show it to Chomsky, and he let Chomsky read it. Before publishing the book, I edited out most of the insults and cracks, but, as far as I know, Chomsky has never read the printed version. So the book has led to quite a lot of personal bitterness between us."

I ask him if he thinks that some scholars might be temperamentally antipathetic to Chomsky's theory.

"Personalities are an impediment to the study of a scientific, technical discipline like linguistics," he says. "Results supposedly obtained through scientific investigation can't be put on a personal basis. It should be not a matter of anyone's likes and dislikes but a matter of which theory fits the facts and which method is more scientific. But the transformationalists have developed a personality cult in linguistics. They have rejected the scientific approach to the study of the human mind and human behavior, and retreated into mysticism, into a sort of medieval scholasticism." His voice rises in pitch. "It's pretty obvious that Chomsky's researches consist primarily in finding a pedigree for his transformational doctrines. His historical work is spotty, and those who know anything about Western intellectual history find all sorts of holes in his interpretations. It's not surprising—questionable scientific method and questionable scholarship go hand in hand."

I ask him why it is, in his opinion, that transformational grammar has received so much attention.

He reflects for some time, and just as I am beginning to think that he has forgotten the question, he says, "Since the Second World War, Western society has tended to make science a scapegoat for the threat of nuclear destruction. It has tended to confuse genuine science with mere technology and to blame our lack of control of technology upon the methods of science. Chomsky epitomizes this trend. To prove his theory of language, he postulates certain entities that cannot be confirmed by the empirical method."

"Wouldn't Chomsky say that your idea of empiricism is rather narrow?" I ask.

"I know we wouldn't have much science if we didn't explain observable things in terms of non-observable things," he says. "But the trouble with Chomsky is that he resorts to a dualistic terminology of mind and body. He is a mentalist. No good scientist talks about mind."

"Don't psychologists talk about mind all the time?" I ask.

"Psychologists do a hell of a lot of things they shouldn't do," he says.

I ask him if he has any other objections to Chomsky's theory.

Again he puffs at his pipe for a time before answering. "In a field like linguistics, which is not very well developed, it's easy to win kudos by rejecting simple old explanations and coming up with abstruse new theories," he says, at last. "This makes you look brave, because you are attacking something supposedly very difficult."

"Do you really think this is what Chomsky is doing?" I ask.

"Not consciously," he says. "But a good scientist shouldn't be blind to evidence that might contradict his theory."

"What kind of evidence do you have in mind?" I ask.

"Well, for example, Chomsky rejects our theory of analogy—that human beings produce new sentences automatically by the processes of analogy, blending, and editing—without making clear quite why he rejects it," he says. "If you look at a cheap dictionary, you'll find that it often defines words in terms of one another—'a' means 'b,' 'b' means 'c,' 'c' means 'a.' In the end, you find that you haven't learned anything. Now, if you try to track down Chomsky's objections to the theory of analogy you'll have the same experience. If you pursue his argument through all the cross-references, you find that his reasoning is circular."

"Do you yourself find the theory of analogy an adequate explanation for the creative use of language?" I ask.

"I think a theory can be wrong and still be useful," he says genially. "In fact, I have a term for it—the productive wrong decision. After chemistry broke away from alchemy, chemists formulated the hypothesis that transmutation was impossible. Although they were wrong, they were able to do productive work on the basis of that hypothesis for a long time. My personal experience, however, has led me to believe that the theory of analogy is correct. I compose music as a hobby, and there is considerable kinship between the operation of producing a sentence or a paragraph and the operation of producing a musical composition. I can see the process of creation and the mechanisms involved writ large when I try to create something that takes a lot of hard, conscious trial and error, and I think that when we're just talking, we're doing the same thing, except that we're doing it much faster and with less editing and rejection, reëditing, and so forth. In fact, music shows traces of being a derivative of language, although it doesn't have certain features of design that language has—for example, it doesn't have semanticity."

I ask him where he would place himself in the linguistic tradition.

He refills his pipe and lights it. "Of course, I'm a structural linguist and I'm a physicalist," he says. "My position is that the behavior of an organism is tied up with its physical structure. We human beings all share certain anatomical features, we all eat, we all breathe, we are all subject to certain natural laws. Because we are all human, all our languages are bound to be somewhat alike. But transformationalists forget that linguistic universals can be only guesses. As you know from reading 'The State of the Art,' my basic philosophical objection to Chomsky's theory has to do with the mathematical concept of well-defined and ill-defined systems. The point here is that the issues that linguists are tinkering with go beyond linguistics into the field of anthropology, biology, physics, and philosophy. In human experience, there are two kinds of systems—well-defined and ill-defined. For well-defined systems we can formulate rules that, if they are applied correctly, will accurately predict results, but for ill-defined systems we cannot do this. The hunk of stuff we call numerals, for instance, is a well-defined system. We have an unlimited series of signs in written notation, and this guarantees that no matter how large a numeral we write, we can always write a larger one. Numbers—the collection of things out there—on the other hand, are an ill-defined system. We represent them by numerals, but numbers exist independently of our representations of them; a hundred stars would still be a hundred stars even if we had no numerals to represent that number of stars with. I think that in the present state of our knowledge all physical phenomena fall into the category of ill-defined systems." He relights his pipe. "If one assumes that one well-defined system can be derived only from another well-defined system, then one must conclude that well-defined systems, like ill-defined systems, have always existed. In other words, one must assume that at creation, instead of mind and matter, there was an ill-defined system, the physical universe, and a well-defined system, the logical universe. But I myself don't think that well-defined systems have been here since the creation. I think that they are the product of human beings, who themselves are ill-defined systems. Human language is a well-defined system if it was created by man. It is an ill-defined system if it was created at the same time as man, as part of his evolutionary heritage. What we scholars have learned about language in the course of a hundred and fifty years of backbreaking work persuades me that language is an ill-defined system, and that it is part of the total physical human experience that has made it possible for man to invent well-defined systems in the first place. Implicit in everything Chomsky does, however, is the assumption that language is a well-defined system, and that our heads are simply so many black boxes with inputs and outputs. In short, either you believe that human life is the product of two different systems or you believe in the purely Platonic, idealistic position that only well-defined systems really exist and all ill-defined systems are shadows—illusions of the well-defined system."

Hockett seems to me to be offering an argument as deductive as he claims Chomsky's is, and I wonder whether his eagerness to demolish Chomsky hasn't led him to espouse ideas that are, in their own way, as debatable as those he is attacking. In any event, I find it hard to believe that his objections are the most devastating ones that could be raised against Chomsky's theory. I ask him how he happened to find himself in the role of Chomsky's chief critic.

"I knew at the start that it would be an uneven battle—just me on one side and Chomsky and all his followers on the other," he says. "But what alternative did I have—to defy all the scientists from Newton to Oppenheimer? The logical conclusion of Chomsky's theory of language was the rejection of the entire scientific tradition of the West."

"By the way, have you ever met Chomsky?" I ask.

"I've met him a few times, but always in a room full of people," he says. "He was always talking—he seemed pleasant and mild-mannered—and I listened to him and offered an occasional comment. But I avoid meeting him now. I figure I've done my bit for traditional linguistics by writing 'The State of the Art.' I've got better things to do than spend the rest of my life fighting a rearguard action against the Philistines."

Before leaving, I ask him to tell me a little about himself.

"I got my B.A. and M.A. in ancient history at Ohio State University, and in 1939 I got my Ph.D. in anthropology from Yale," he says. "I worked on Chinese with the Army during the war, and my first job at Cornell, in 1946, was teaching elementary Chinese as well as linguistics. My wife teaches mathematics at Ithaca College. Before that, she taught it at Cornell off and on for twenty years. We have four daughters and one son, and all of them are musical. Number One—she's married—is a professional oboist and pianist. Numbers Two, Three, and Four all took piano lessons, but I think only Number Four will keep up her music. She is very good on the flute. Number Five—she's seventeen—plays cello and bassoon, a strange combination but a very useful one."

Roman Jakobson, who has been described by Chomsky as "the elder statesman of linguistics" and by Hockett as "a great guy," was born in Russia in 1896 and has lived in the United States since 1941. He is a linguist in the old tradition of scholarship—an authority on phonology and morphology, on metric patterns in Indo-European languages, on the Prince Igor tale and other Slavic epics, and on Russian and Czech experimental poetry—and has written books and articles in Russian, French, German, and English. I go to see him in

Cambridge, Massachusetts, where he teaches part time at M.I.T., and where he lives in semi-retirement with his wife, a specialist in Russian literature, who is known professionally as Dr. Krystyna Pomorska, and whom he married in 1962. Their house, set back from the street, is an old wooden one with a fence around it—the typical residence of a successful professor in Cambridge. Jakobson greets me at the door. He is a strong-looking man of average height, with eyes of an almost celestial blue. His left eye looks to the side. He is clean-shaven, with thick graying hair, and he is dressed in a blue blazer decorated with a Legion of Honor ribbon, a blue shirt open at the collar, gray slacks, and brown moccasins. With a courtly flourish, he ushers me into the house and shows me through a hall containing a piano, then into an antechamber, and then down a few steps into his study, which is a long room with French doors opening onto a small, unkempt garden. In the study, there are several comfortable yellow armchairs, a yellow carpet, and a Scandinavian desk. The walls are wood-panelled, and are hung with a few drawings by Russian modernists. All around are bookcases filled with old, rare-looking editions of grammars and old, rare-looking icons. Some of the icons are primitives; one is of a tree of life with birds in its spreading branches. Some are more elaborate; one is an image of Hell shown in concentric circles as the intestines of a demonic figure. Looking down from the tops of the bookcases are Slavic toys and puppets; here and there are painted antique dishes.

"Most of my books, so to say, live in my office at M.I.T.," Jakobson tells me. "Only precious books are here, or books, so to say, on topics of my current interest. I am just now finishing a study of the relation between liturgical poetry and music in the Slavic world of the ninth century. But I am not being faithful to any one subject for very long, or I become, so to say, an automaton." With a sweep of his hand, he indicates the icons, and he continues, "These icons I am collecting on my travels. I had a collection of icons in Russia when I was a young boy, but I lost it during the Revolution. I had another collection in Czechoslovakia, but I lost it, too, after the German occupation."

Jakobson speaks English with a Russian intonation, and often in broken sentences, using "so to say" as a crutch, and his manner is very European, old-fashioned, and melodramatic, with much waving of the hands and much scooping up chunks of air, as if he were a conductor. Ceremoniously, he offers me a chair, and then he pulls up a straight-backed, rush-bottomed chair for himself.

"Do you do most of your work here?" I ask.

"You will probably laugh, but I do most of my work when I am away from Cambridge, preferably on some quiet island," he says. "Recently, I was on an island in Georgia that belongs to friends of mine. It is virgin forest—there are only a couple of houses—and it is wonderfully quiet and a good place to work."

"Do you keep very busy, then, here in Cambridge?"

"Friends are always coming from other countries to visit us," he says. "Hattori, the leading Japanese linguist, just stayed with us. Tomorrow, Rosetti, the leading Rumanian linguist, is coming here to stay. I must welcome all these linguists, because whenever I go to their countries they are welcoming me. A couple of weeks ago, I met Noam, and he said it was a shame we hadn't seen each other for such a long time. We took our diaries out and found that he was busy then and then, and I was busy then and then. And so it goes."

He asks me a few questions about myself and listens to my answers intently, assuming an expression of deep concentration—his eyebrows going down and to-gether—that resembles sorrow or anger.

Then I ask him how many languages he speaks.

"This is very difficult to answer, this question," he says. "It depends what means 'speak.' I can improvise lectures in Russian, Czech, Polish, French, German, and English—six languages. Kurylowicz, the leading Polish linguist, once said, 'Jakobson is a peculiar man. He speaks fluently Russian in six languages.' Here in my English you have the proof." He laughs. "For me, the most important thing about knowing a language is, so to say, to be able to make yourself understood. If one begins to have little doubts about one's pronunciation, and so on, and tries to improve, one can eventually do it, but in the process it weakens—for me, at least—the best capacity for improvising. I think the best way to become a polyglot is to know as a child more than one language. When I was six or seven years old, I was equally fluent in Russian and French."

"What language do you speak here at home?" I ask.

"My wife is Polish, and we speak Polish at home," he says. "Also sometimes Russian. Both my wife and I read more languages than we speak. I can read about twenty-five—nearly all the Western European languages and nearly all the Slavic languages—and I am acquainted with the Scandinavian languages, though I've forgotten them. But how many I read depends on whether you mean by 'read' reading poetry, which is much more difficult than reading, so to say, scientific literature. In my book 'Poetry of Grammar and Grammar of Poetry' I analyze poems in about twenty languages, but I couldn't read them on the subway. I hate to boast, but I have a knack for understanding poetry. I scarcely know Japanese, but when I was in Japan recently I analyzed an eighth-century Japanese poem before a large Japanese audience."

"Does Russian still have the greatest hold on you?" I ask.

"It depends on what you mean by 'hold,' " he says. "I like to speculate about the languages polyglots think and dream in. For me, the language doesn't depend on the characters I'm conversing with in the dream but on the topic and, so to say, its emotional atmosphere. In dreams, I am speaking Czech with Englishmen. Polyglots are a peculiar breed. They even have two special kinds of aphasia. In one kind, one forgets all the languages except one's mother tongue, even if one hasn't used the mother tongue since childhood. I once spent some time in the hospital in New York, and I saw many cases of this kind; elderly Jews who had been in different kinds of accidents had forgotten completely English and begun talking Yiddish, which they hadn't spoken for years, and which their families didn't understand. In the other kind of aphasia, one forgets all languages except the one with the greatest emotional associations. There is a famous story of an old Frenchwoman who fell from a horse and suddenly could speak only Italian. She had had an unhappy love affair with an Italian in her youth." He nods sympathetically. "I often used to wonder what would happen to me if I fell from a horse. I didn't quite fall from a horse, but I had a terrible motor accident twenty-one years ago. I almost lost my legs. It's a very strange story. It was during a snowstorm not far from Poughkeepsie, in New York. I was driving with a student, and I was thrown from the car. I was lying in the snow waiting for an ambulance. Every sentence I uttered, the student later told me, I repeated in several languages: 'Gentlemen, help me!' *'Herrshaften, helfen Sie mir!'* *'Messieurs, aidez-moi!'* These shifts from one language to another, you know, are completely automatized in me."

I ask him how he became interested in linguistics.

"I owe my interest not so much to the teaching of linguists and scholars as to the inspiration of the great artists of my youth—Picasso, Braque, Le Corbusier, Joyce, and Stravinsky, and the great Russian poet Khlebnikov. Khlebnikov was a remarkable experimental poet. You know, I like this expression of Maurice Bowra—'experimental poetry.' I decided when I was at school that I would become a linguist. My father was a chemist, and he asked me, 'Roman, why have you decided to become a linguist?' And I said, 'Linguistics is no different from chemistry. I want to find the finite elementary units in the structure of linguistic elements.' I studied linguistics in Moscow, also in St. Petersburg, and, later, in Prague. I became very much attached to a scholar who was a little older than I was, Nicholas Trubetzkoy, and in the late twenties he and I, along with one or two friends, founded the Prague Circle, an informal intellectual group, which became, so to say, the center of the European structural-linguistics movement. In fact, I can boast that I was the first to use the term 'structural linguistics.' From the beginning, Trubetzkoy and I came into contact with the leading American linguists of the time—Sapir and Bloomfield and Benjamin Lee Whorf—through our publications and correspondence. Trubetzkoy died in 1938, and I left Europe and came to the United States as a refugee in 1941. At first, I was at the École Libre in New York. This was a university founded by French scholars who were refugees from the Nazi Occupation. We were teachers and students of one another. I introduced Claude Lévi-Strauss to linguistics, and he introduced me to anthropology. Later, I taught at Columbia, then at Harvard. I have trained many of the linguists teaching in America today. I counted once—about a hundred of my former students are professors in this country. Chomsky, Halle, Hockett—all have attended my lectures. Recently, I was at the University of Chicago. I was surrounded by former students of mine in general linguistics, poetics, Slavic philology, and linguistic redundancy. So it is at most of the universities. My real love is, so to say, the Slavic Middle Ages, but recently I've been working on the connections between linguistics, science, and the humanities, on the one hand, and language and other sign systems, on the other. I don't think one can have a

theory of language without studying other sign systems—painting, sculpture, cinema, theatre, music,
pantomime. All must be taken into account." He finishes
emphatically, raising his left palm over his head and
striking it with his right fist.

I turn the conversation to transformational grammar
and ask him how he regards Chomsky's work.

"Philosophically, I think his most important contribution is his answer to the behaviorist, physicalist,
mechanist approach to language," he says. "He has revived the discredited mentalist approach to language,
and this is of value to linguistics. Technically, his most
important contribution has been his work on syntax.
Before Chomsky, linguists did not sufficiently take into
account the way in which we select one syntactic structure over another. The structural linguists concerned
themselves only with areas in which the speaker has little
latitude, like phonology and morphology. Chomsky revived and developed the notion of hierarchy in syntax
and reopened the problem of creative language use. I
don't want to diminish Noam's contribution, but he and
his epigones think that the first business of linguists is to
sketch out all the grammatical rules, and that metre,
style, and everything else are not worth bothering
with." He throws his hands about like a boxer. "I have
many other criticisms. Chomsky's epigones often know
only one language—English—and they draw all their
examples from it. They say, for instance, that 'beautiful
girl' is a transformation of 'girl who is beautiful,' and yet
in some languages there is no such thing as a subordinate
clause or 'who is.' Their claim that the imperative is a

transformation of the simple declarative is nonsense. 'Go' is not necessarily a transformation of 'You will go.' 'Go' is an imperative, and a child may learn the imperative 'Go' long before he learns 'You will go.' It is nonsense to say, as they say, that every sentence is spoken for the first time. Many, many sentences are simply, so to say, repeats of one another. The notion of hierarchy in syntax is not new with Chomsky and his epigones. Our Prague Circle was working with the notion of marked and unmarked forms as early as 1930. We postulated then that there was a whole hierarchy of these syntactic forms, ranging from the least characterized and specified, the unmarked form, to the most characterized and specified, the marked form. For instance, in morphology the present tense is vaster and less marked than the past tense. You can use the present tense to describe something that happened in the past. You can say 'Caesar crosses the Rubicon.' But you can't use the past tense to describe something that is happening in the present or the future. You can't say 'I went to New York' when you are just setting off for New York. In phonology, a plural is a marked form; a singular is unmarked. But our Prague Circle applied the idea of marked and unmarked forms only to morphology and phonology. Chomsky carried this idea over to syntax and made it much more, so to say, palpable with his terms 'deep structure' and 'surface structure.' "

"Do you agree, then, with Chomsky's conceptions of deep structure and surface structure?" I ask.

"I think the concept has an important kernel of truth," he says. "But it carries a danger of absolutism. In linguistics, we must all remain relativists and insist that there is no clear-cut opposition between deep and surface structures but only a hierarchy of deeper and less deep structures. The very fact that Chomsky and his epigones postulate a whole hierarchy of intermediate structures is an indication to me that there is no such thing as absolute deep structure and absolute surface structure. The more Chomsky's epigones talk about deep structure, the more remote and incomprehensible it gets. Pushkin once said about the metaphysical poets, 'The nearer they got to Heaven, the colder it was.' The same can be said of the epigones."

"What do you think of Hockett's criticisms of Chomsky?" I ask.

"It is very difficult for me to know what Hockett's position on any question is," he says. "He changes his mind every day. Hockett says that he is a Bloomfieldian, but Bloomfield was a great friend of mine, and he once said to me, 'There are many people who say that they are Bloomfieldians. I can tell you what the common denominator of all Bloomfieldians is—they don't understand Bloomfield.' I agree with what Bloomfield once said to me about Hockett: 'He is a linguistic craftsman, and it is very dangerous for a mere craftsman to enter into theoretical discussions.' "

I ask him how he would assess the contribution of transformational grammar to linguistics.

"The transformationalists say that there is no topic worth studying in linguistics except transformational grammar," he says. "Linguistics is a vast field. It is among the oldest of the sciences. The first scientific grammar was written by the Sumerians. And interesting work is being done today in many areas of linguistics and in many countries. But it's hard to judge the contribution, so to say, of people who are still alive and working. I could name a number of great linguists who in their lifetimes were known only to a handful of scholars and who yet changed the study of linguistics. I could also name some enormously popular linguists who eventually proved to be completely unimportant. I've heard it said in this country first that the real study of linguistics began with Sapir, then that it began with Whorf, then that it began with Bloomfield, then that it began with Chomsky. Now I hear it said that it has begun with certain of Chomsky's epigones. People always like to exaggerate the novelty of their theory when they're launching it. It's exactly like the advertising for a new brand of cigarette, so to say—'Never a flavor so rich. Never a taste so smooth.' I would say about the transformationalists as a group what I said about the so-called Bloomfieldians when they were riding high—that in this country there is a danger with everything of mass-producing from a single model. So it was with the models of linguistic description that the Bloomfieldians reproduced, and so it is now with the transformations that Chomsky's epigones are marketing. I think it was Alfred de Musset who said once that only a provincial schoolteacher believes that there exist absolutely new ideas."

Over the years, I have followed many debates among contemporary intellectuals. Sometimes, when I have been weighing the pros and cons of the debaters' arguments, my head has become a vast parliament of modern ideologues, each faction advocating its own particular program but all of them agreeing that perhaps, in our democratic, fragmented era, truth can emerge only from the clash of ideas, and even of personalities. After talking with other linguists at other universities, I weigh in my mind the debate over transformational grammar and read into the record of my mental parliament a few paragraphs from the notes I've jotted down along the way.

CHOMSKY'S SCHOOL: His theoretical house in disarray. One source of confusion whether meaning of sentence expressed in terms of deep structure, or deep structure itself meaning. Have talk at M.I.T. Faculty Club, over dinner and wine, with Janet Fodor, Oxford philosopher now doing research in the Linguistics Department of M.I.T., married to American, Jerry Fodor, describing himself as "psycholinguist." "When the cat's away, the mice will play, and while Chomsky was away at Berkeley for a semester giving his famous lectures, John Ross, at M.I.T., and George Lakoff, at Harvard, seized the opportunity to put across their ideas about deep structure," she says. "They postulated a much more abstract deep structure for a sentence than Chomsky did, and, consequently, made their transformations do much more work. Their famous example was 'Floyd broke the glass,' of which they said the deep structure was 'It happened that Floyd did Floyd caused that the glass became broken.' 'Did' because all action verbs have embedded in them the verb 'do.' When Chomsky came back, he said that Lakoff and Ross were producing deep structures that were not syntactic but semantic. He didn't deny that 'Floyd broke the glass' could be made more explicit in, say, 'Floyd caused the glass to become broken,' but he said that the meaning was derived semantically. The argument is still raging, and other young linguists have joined in. Very often the debate turns not on any evidence—for there really isn't any evidence yet—but on intuitions of grammaticality. Lakoff, who is now at the University of Michigan, is busy setting up a rival camp out there and storing up ammunition to demolish Chomsky. Once, Chomsky was a revolutionary. Now he has been forced into the position of a conservative."

LINGUISTICS: Most universities throughout world still in establishment tradition. Still teaching liturgies of philological facts—Old English 'o' pronounced 'ah' below the Humber, and Old English 'ah' pronounced 'o' above the Humber. But Chomsky a popular phenomenon. Also, one philologist says, "It's a remote possibility, but he may have cracked language wide open; he holds out a promise of an underlying system to language." But there are other movements in linguistics; e.g., those of Jean Piaget, in Switzerland, and André Martinet, in France, each with an influential school of his own.

PHILOSOPHY: Just received letter from Oxford philosopher friend telling how Oxford philosophers, renowned for sharp intellects, treated Chomsky when he gave Locke Lectures: "The lectures were given at the Schools in the afternoon, and he filled the Schools as probably no one had done since Bertrand Russell. How many people turned up to hear Chomsky because of the pull of his linguistic theory and how many because of his espousal of radical politics, which are sweeping through Oxford like a hurricane at the moment, I leave for you to judge. The lectures were about language and mind—another version of the ones he gave at Berkeley. After each one of them, a group of us, about twenty-five professors, Fellows, and postgraduate students, including P. F. Strawson, Gilbert Ryle, Elizabeth Anscombe, and Julie Rountree, who has succeeded Philippa Foot as a Fellow at Somerville—all the great philosophical lights—and younger chaps like Jonathan Cohen and Brian Loar, would meet with Chomsky for a discussion session in a small lecture hall around the corner. After dinner, an even smaller group of us, consisting of Strawson, Miss Anscombe, Julie Rountree, Brian Loar, and two or three other people, would meet in Strawson's rooms at Magdalen. I remember that on at least one occasion Peter Geach was there. After all these years of watching him, I still can't quite tell whether he is asleep or awake behind his closed eyes. Our main interest, as you can imagine, was in the validity of some of Chomsky's claims about innate schematism, and the kind of linguistic evidence he could produce to support them. Miss Anscombe once asked him in what sense he thought innate schematisms were in the mind—what he thought the mind was like, and how any schematism or any other thing could really be in it—and Chomsky's reply was to trot out the same old examples: 'John is easy to please,' 'John is eager to please.' People like Miss Anscombe—though she was being immensely charming, for Miss Anscombe—I don't think were really terribly interested, while people like

Strawson seemed to think that Chomsky really had got hold of something, but they couldn't make out quite what." Even if Chomsky had a deeper knowledge of philosophy, he would not change theory of language, because most of his work is in syntax and phonology and has nothing to do with philosophy. Perhaps his philosophical ideas only a flower on top of his real technical work in linguistics.

NINTH ANNUAL NEW YORK UNIVERSITY INSTITUTE OF PHILOSOPHY REVISITED: Goodman answers Chomsky's rebuttal: "I plead guilty to the charge of ignorance of most of current linguistic theory. . . . Such ignorance probably explains why I can never follow the argument that starts from interesting differences in behavior between parallel phrases such as 'eager to please' and 'easy to please'; that characterizes these differences as matters of 'deep' rather than 'surface' structure; and that moves on to innate ideas. The extent of my obtuseness will be underlined if I remark that also 'cat' and 'rat,' like 'eager' and 'easy,' are similar in many ways, and that certain parallel longer expressions in which they are embedded behave quite disparately. 'Cattle' is plural, 'rattle' is singular. There is such a thing as a rattling but not such a thing as a cattling. And while rattles rattle, cattle do not cattle; that is, just as we can 'nominalize' 'eager to please' but not 'easy to please,' so we can 'verbalize' 'rattle' but not 'cattle.' Are all these peculiarities 'deep' as contrasted with the difference between 'cat' and 'rat'? I am not denying that the case of 'eager' and 'easy' may have important features not shared by the case of 'cat' and 'rat.' I am asking for the grounds for the inference from such features, or from any other peculiarities in the behavior of words, to innate ideas."

On this inconclusive note, the parliament is adjourned until the next sitting.

1971